Tract_landscape architects and planners

tract   and planners

landscape architects

Haig Beck and Jackie Cooper_Introduction essays by Professor David Yencken, Peter Walker, Professor RD Gibson and Garry Emery

Published in Australia in 2004 by The Images Publishing Group Pty Ltd ABN 89 059 734 431

6 Bastow Place, Mulgrave, Victoria, 3170, Australia Telephone +61 3 9561 5544 Facsimile +61 3 9561 4860

Email books@images.com.au Website www.imagespublishinggroup.com

Copyright © The Images Publishing Group Pty Ltd 2004. The Images Publishing Group reference number 358

National Library of Australia. Cataloguing-in-Publication entry: Beck, Haig. Tract. ISBN 1 876907 36 3.

1. Tract Consultants Australia 2. Landscape architectural firms – Australia 3. Landscape architecture – Australia.

I. Cooper, Jackie II. Title.

712.06094

Edited by Jackie Cooper. Designed by Emery Frost

Film by Mission Productions. Printed by Everbest Printing Co. Ltd. in Hong Kong/China

IMAGES has included on its website a page for special notices in relation to this and our other publications. Please visit this site
www.imagespublishinggroup.com

Contents

landscape architecture

economics
environmental
modern australia

social culture

modernism

planning

In 1973, when Tract was first established, landscape practice, as envisaged by Frederick Law Olmsted and other great landscape pioneers, was little evident in Australia. Olmsted was a designer of rare talent as his design for Central Park in New York illustrates. He was a landscape planner of perception and great strategic skill as is shown by his open space plans for New York and other cities. He was a nature conservationist who played a large part in bringing the Yosemite National Park into being. He and Vaux also coined the term 'landscape architect' which they envisaged as spanning all these activities and more. It was only later that planning spun off as a separate discipline in its own right. Nevertheless, the relationships between landscape design and planning and urban design have remained central to the profession in its mature form.

Australia has had many able landscape designers. In 1975, the death of Ellis Stones, one such designer, was the main trigger for the creation of Tract. Edna Walling, Ellis Stones's mentor, was an even finer designer. Going back further still, William Guilfoyle's designs for Melbourne's Royal Botanic Gardens and other great country gardens have been justly praised around the world. Thus Australia has not lacked talented designers. What it lacked in the early 1970s were practices that combined landscape design and planning in their many different forms and thus practices that were able to extend the role of landscape practice in both the public and private domain.

The three original principals brought some special characteristics to Tract. Howard McCorkell was an urban planner, Rodney Wulff a landscape planner and designer with considerable formal skills and Steve Calhoun a talented and intuitive designer. Two were Australian and one was American. All, however, had studied overseas in courses not available in Australia at the time: Howard at Edinburgh University, Rodney at Oregon and Harvard and later at Cornell for his PhD and Steve at Iowa State and the Graduate School of Design at Harvard. Furthermore, all had worked for international firms of distinction such as Colin Buchanan in England and Sasaki Walker in the USA. There was no comparable practice group in Australia at the time and it was a very long time before groups with similar arrays of skills would appear. When they did eventually appear they were often associated with overseas firms. Surveying the scene in the mid-1970s, Howard, Rodney and Steve were dismayed at what they saw. At that time in Australia there was little recognition of the role that could be played by imaginative landscape planning and design. Corporations saw little value in landscape architecture. Local governments had few if any employees who thought of urban and landscape design as strategic tools for the enrichment of their localities. Government authorities did not consider that design had much to do with their responsibilities except in relation to public buildings. Architects assumed it was their right to be responsible for any urban design work that was available and when they obtained large commissions rarely if ever considered working in partnership with landscape architects. In the beginning, Tract struggled for survival, since the only work immediately available was coming from Merchant Builders, the host organisation that had brought Tract into being. This work, involving an unusual collaboration of highly talented architects, planners, landscape, interior and graphic designers, won many design awards in which Tract actively shared. However this was not enough to support the fledgling Tract.

Professor David Yencken AO_Tract founder's perspective

David Yencken began his working life with a small gallery devoted to Australian painting. He pioneered motels when there were none in Australia, working with John Mockridge and Robin Boyd, two pre-eminent architects of their times. Together with John Ridge he assembled an array of outstanding architects, landscape architects, interior designers and graphic designers for the project housing firm Merchant Builders. When later head of the Ministry of Planning and Environment, he was responsible for dramatic urban design changes in Melbourne. These projects won very many design awards. He was Chairman of the Australian Heritage Commission for six years and subsequently Professor and Head of the School of Environmental Planning, University of Melbourne. David Yencken was also the founder of Tract Consultants and its managing director in its first few years. The two great passions of his working life have been design and the environment, about which he has written widely.

The Tract office was located on Fitzroy Street, St Kilda, a bohemian bayside inner suburb of Melbourne. At the bottom of the street lay Catani Gardens and a foreshore that ran for kilometres in both directions. St Kilda and its beaches had fallen into decay by the 1970s. Steve, Rodney and Howard saw an opportunity to employ their skills on a civic scale and be the catalyst for a revival of one of Melbourne's most interesting suburbs.

The Tract plan called for land reclamation measures that would restore the sand to the beaches, clean up derelict buildings, remove car parks and create a foreshore parkland. The most controversial proposal was for extensive plantings of Canary Island palms, Norfolk pines and Moreton Bay figs. There were remnant survivors of these species in evidence along the foreshore. The Tract plan called for these trees to be planted in extensive avenues to link remnant pockets and give continuity to the foreshore and city beyond. A far-sighted city engineer, Martin Verhoeven, coaxed the city council into accepting the plan. Most of the plan is now in place and has helped St Kilda enjoy an impressive renaissance. The St Kilda foreshore project put Tract on its feet. The many projects that followed have included strategic planning and sub-regional studies such as at Falls Creek; masterplanning such as the Newcastle Harbour Foreshore; many site planning and urban design projects such as Melbourne's Southbank; and very many site and garden designs. This by no means covers the full extent of Tract's work but does give some sense of it. As the work expanded, new partners and staff with different skills were brought into Tract.

Tract's achievement is firstly, that its work has consistently been of a high standard. It has, secondly, enlarged the scope of landscape architecture in Australia and elsewhere. A firm introducing new practices and doing good work over a long period of time is a wonderful challenge to others to do as well or better. Rodney Wulff and Steve Calhoun have also devoted a large amount of time and effort to university landscape programmes. They were together largely responsible for establishing the first professional degree course at RMIT and are today visiting professors at the University of Melbourne. The influence of Tract has therefore been threefold.

The body of work that Tract, and subsequently others, has carried out has opened the eyes of public bodies and private clients to the potential of landscape practice. Today the recognition of that potential is light years away from the recognition given to it in the early 1970s.

Since 1950 the field of landscape architecture has seen tremendous growth and change. The rapid post-war expansion of urban and suburban areas has posed problems, some unique to various countries, but many common throughout the world. Through individual practices and through teaching and research in universities, the field has attempted to find order, beauty and ecological balance. Our collective and sequential experiences define our progress and inform our continued efforts. However, certain firms in certain places have made exceptional contributions to these efforts and Tract is one of these firms.

In 1956 Hideo Sasaki at the Harvard Graduate School of Design and in his then new office in Watertown, Massachusetts, began to try to reassemble the field of landscape architecture based on his understanding of the original Olmstedian model that had included both the fields of landscape design and city planning. Over the next ten years he gathered together at the school and at his office a collection of talented young practitioners of landscape architecture, planning, civil engineering, and architecture working together in true collaboration on what he then termed 'site planning'. Sasaki felt that this reorganisation of modern landscape architecture was required in order to respond to the immense demands of the post-war world for expanded facilities for education, recreation, transportation, housing and urban growth.

Rodney Wulff and Steve Calhoun were both trained at the HGSD, and Steve, through his practice at Sasaki Walker Associates, was exposed to these ideas and new organisations and to the vast environmental problems Sasaki's reorganisation was meant to address. In 1973 under the far-sighted and ambitious sponsorship of David Yencken, founder of Merchant Builders, the office of Tract was formed in Melbourne. The ideas and ideals they brought to this new practice were at that time also new to the practice of landscape architecture in Australia.

Over the past thirty years Tract has been involved in almost all of the types of major land-use changes that have so challenged the aesthetic, functional, and social environment in which we live. First in Melbourne, and then as success came throughout Australia, it has struggled with the urban and suburban housing explosion, the almost unmanageable expansion in the facilities for elementary and college education, and new recreation demands that reach from primeval preservation through neighbourhood greenways and parks. Its work includes new urban outdoor areas of many sizes and purposes including urban renewal, brownfield renovation, waterway designs and management, as well as wildlife studies, and all forms of transportation including automobile, pedestrian, linear bike-ways and systems of extended jogging trails.

Peter Walker has had a significant impact on the field of landscape architecture over a four-decade career, crystallising what is known as the American corporate multidisciplinary office. Educated at Berkeley and the Harvard Design School, Walker has taught, lectured, written, and served as an adviser to numerous public agencies, while exerting tight control over the design of his own projects.

The scope of his landscape inquiries is expansive as well as deep. Projects range from small gardens to new cities, from urban plazas to corporate headquarters and academic campuses. With a dedicated concern for urban and environmental issues, his designs shape the landscape in a variety of geographic and cultural contexts, from the United States to Japan, China, Australia, and Europe. Walker is also the founder of Spacemaker Press and his work has been extensively published in Europe and Asia as well as the United States.

The Tract office was located on Fitzroy Street, St Kilda, a bohemian bayside inner suburb of Melbourne. At the bottom of the street lay Catani Gardens and a foreshore that ran for kilometres in both directions. St Kilda and its beaches had fallen into decay by the 1970s. Steve, Rodney and Howard saw an opportunity to employ their skills on a civic scale and be the catalyst for a revival of one of Melbourne's most interesting suburbs.

The Tract plan called for land reclamation measures that would restore the sand to the beaches, clean up derelict buildings, remove car parks and create a foreshore parkland. The most controversial proposal was for extensive plantings of Canary Island palms, Norfolk pines and Moreton Bay figs. There were remnant survivors of these species in evidence along the foreshore. The Tract plan called for these trees to be planted in extensive avenues to link remnant pockets and give continuity to the foreshore and city beyond. A far-sighted city engineer, Martin Verhoeven, coaxed the city council into accepting the plan. Most of the plan is now in place and has helped St Kilda enjoy an impressive renaissance. The St Kilda foreshore project put Tract on its feet. The many projects that followed have included strategic planning and sub-regional studies such as at Falls Creek; masterplanning such as the Newcastle Harbour Foreshore; many site planning and urban design projects such as Melbourne's Southbank; and very many site and garden designs. This by no means covers the full extent of Tract's work but does give some sense of it. As the work expanded, new partners and staff with different skills were brought into Tract.

Tract's achievement is firstly, that its work has consistently been of a high standard. It has, secondly, enlarged the scope of landscape architecture in Australia and elsewhere. A firm introducing new practices and doing good work over a long period of time is a wonderful challenge to others to do as well or better. Rodney Wulff and Steve Calhoun have also devoted a large amount of time and effort to university landscape programmes. They were together largely responsible for establishing the first professional degree course at RMIT and are today visiting professors at the University of Melbourne. The influence of Tract has therefore been threefold.

The body of work that Tract, and subsequently others, has carried out has opened the eyes of public bodies and private clients to the potential of landscape practice. Today the recognition of that potential is light years away from the recognition given to it in the early 1970s.

Since 1950 the field of landscape architecture has seen tremendous growth and change. The rapid post-war expansion of urban and suburban areas has posed problems, some unique to various countries, but many common throughout the world. Through individual practices and through teaching and research in universities, the field has attempted to find order, beauty and ecological balance. Our collective and sequential experiences define our progress and inform our continued efforts. However, certain firms in certain places have made exceptional contributions to these efforts and Tract is one of these firms.

In 1956 Hideo Sasaki at the Harvard Graduate School of Design and in his then new office in Watertown, Massachusetts, began to try to reassemble the field of landscape architecture based on his understanding of the original Olmstedian model that had included both the fields of landscape design and city planning. Over the next ten years he gathered together at the school and at his office a collection of talented young practitioners of landscape architecture, planning, civil engineering, and architecture working together in true collaboration on what he then termed 'site planning'. Sasaki felt that this reorganisation of modern landscape architecture was required in order to respond to the immense demands of the post-war world for expanded facilities for education, recreation, transportation, housing and urban growth.

Rodney Wulff and Steve Calhoun were both trained at the HGSD, and Steve, through his practice at Sasaki Walker Associates, was exposed to these ideas and new organisations and to the vast environmental problems Sasaki's reorganisation was meant to address. In 1973 under the far-sighted and ambitious sponsorship of David Yencken, founder of Merchant Builders, the office of Tract was formed in Melbourne. The ideas and ideals they brought to this new practice were at that time also new to the practice of landscape architecture in Australia. Over the past thirty years Tract has been involved in almost all of the types of major land-use changes that have so challenged the aesthetic, functional, and social environment in which we live. First in Melbourne, and then as success came throughout Australia, it has struggled with the urban and suburban housing explosion, the almost unmanageable expansion in the facilities for elementary and college education, and new recreation demands that reach from primeval preservation through neighbourhood greenways and parks. Its work includes new urban outdoor areas of many sizes and purposes including urban renewal, brownfield renovation, waterway designs and management, and all forms of transportation including automobile, pedestrian, linear bike-ways and systems of extended jogging trails.

Peter Walker has had a significant impact on the field of landscape architecture over a four-decade career, crystallising what is known as the American corporate multidisciplinary office. Educated at Berkeley and the Harvard Design School, Walker has taught, lectured, written, and served as an adviser to numerous public agencies, while exerting tight control over the design of his own projects. The scope of his landscape inquiries is expansive as well as deep. Projects range from small gardens to new cities, from urban plazas to corporate headquarters and academic campuses. With a dedicated concern for urban and environmental issues, his designs shape the landscape in a variety of geographic and cultural contexts, from the United States to Japan, China, Australia, and Europe. Walker is also the founder of Spacemaker Press and his work has been extensively published in Europe and Asia as well as the United States.

Tract, as planner, urban designer and landscape architect, has worked together with Australian architects, urban renewal staff, developers and universities and has combined its joint experiences to propose practical and sensitive long-range physical plans that have been and are being implemented in stages over many years.

Tract has developed and refined all these services while gaining the respect of its Australian design peers, resulting in numerous professional awards. Through publication it has become an important professional model throughout Australia and the world.

By its efforts and ingenuity Tract has engaged increasingly large, difficult and interesting challenges and by so doing has made an important design contribution to the beauty and functionality within the modern Australian landscape. For many years, both Steve and Rodney, like Sasaki before them, have shared their ideas and experiences with students through university teaching.

This book, a documentation of many of their important contributions and accomplishments, will be of considerable interest to environmental designers worldwide.

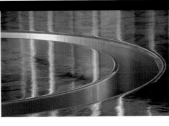

I would like to formally record my appreciation of the contribution that Tract has made to the development of the Gardens Point campus of QUT and the significant impact that this has had on the culture and performance of the University.

Traditionally, the Gardens Point peninsula has always been a place of the people, from the days when its original owners used it as a meeting place and communal space. However, for much of the twentieth century, the changing ownership of the land meant that the campus had evolved as an uncoordinated jumble of buildings and walkways, with no clear plan or vision for its development. Consequently, over the last decade, I have worked with Tract to revisit the traditional focus of the land, and to come up with a vision for its development that was largely focused on recreating the campus as a place of the people. This work has seen a major transformation that takes advantage of the prime positioning of the Gardens Point campus, between the Botanic Gardens and the Brisbane River, along with an upgrading of its facilities to cater for its new occupants – an increasingly sophisticated student population.

The focus of the upgrades has always been our students – we have aimed to enhance services for students, to provide appropriate spaces for research and innovation, and to alleviate overcrowding in teaching and recreational areas. The globalisation of higher education, the impact of new technologies on teaching, the economic imperative of innovation and applied research, and the emergence of Queensland as Australia's 'smart state', have all placed enormous space demands on QUT's physical facilities, particularly at Gardens Point.

At the same time, we have always had in mind the quality of campus life that students still crave as a core ingredient of their university experience. With Tract, we have turned what used to be a stark, sterile, uninviting block of land into one that has outdoor spaces, 'exterior rooms' that make maximum use of Queensland's wonderful climate. One of the major catalysts for this change was the removal of the fence that served as a barrier between the Botanic Gardens and the Main Drive of the campus. This effectively has opened up the whole peninsula, by connecting the campus with the city and its gardens. Students now congregate in droves in outdoor café spaces, gather along Main Drive or drift into the Gardens while they eat their lunches, group together in the Union Square to discuss assignments and work together on research. These activities used to be the province of classrooms and lecture theatres, and our students would desert the campus unless timetables forced them to be here. This is no longer the case.

12_

Professor RD Gibson AO _ A Client's Perspective

Dennis Gibson has been a teacher, researcher and university leader over a forty-year career. He holds degrees including a higher doctorate from three British universities and honorary doctorates from two Australia universities.

He is currently an Emeritus Professor and an Adjunct Professor. Since April 2003 he has been Chancellor of RMIT University in Melbourne; prior to that he was Vice-Chancellor and Chief Executive Officer of QUT and its predecessor QIT in Brisbane. As Vice-Chancellor he emphasised the need to break down cultural and physical barriers between university campuses and the surrounding urban communities.

QUT's relationships with business, commerce and government have always been strong and have always played a significant part in the strategic development of the campus. They have been further strengthened by the opening up of the campus, which in effect has served as a physical reflection of the opening up of QUT to the wider community, the end of the traditional 'walled in' concept of the university as an isolated entity. The systematic transformation of the campus has provided a background which showcases student achievement and other aspects of the university's cultural life, and which has brought a new sense of creativity and harmony to the campus. When one considers the total cost of the capital development that has been undertaken at QUT over the last fifteen years, the landscape component has really only represented a fraction of this cost, yet it has had a positive impact on campus life that has been well out of proportion with the comparatively small amount that has been spent on it.

Tract's vision for Gardens Point has been unfailingly accurate, and has provided us with the opportunity to further develop teaching and research facilities of the highest quality for students, staff and the community, at the same time continuing the transformation of the campus into an environment that blends social and cultural needs with a modern university's requirements. It has been much more than cosmetic – it has transformed the Gardens Point campus of QUT into a modern, integrated environment that has become a pleasure to work and study in. The completion in 2001 of the link to the new Goodwill Bridge has been a further demonstration of the creativity, quality and professionalism that have characterised all of Tract's contributions to this university.

From the window of my office in U block I can see the evidence on a daily basis, as a steady stream of people travel along Main Drive. Thanks to the bridge, we are no longer a cul-de-sac but a vital thoroughfare into the city, and thanks to Tract, we are no longer a sterile place, but a thriving, energetic example of modern university life. This (2002) is my last full year as Vice-Chancellor of QUT and I can honestly say that sharing with Tract the transformation of this campus has been one of the most satisfying highlights of my twenty years here.

My professional relationship with Stephen, Rodney and Howard, the founding partners of Tract with David Yencken, began in 1976 when Steve arrived in Australia from California and promptly invited me to review Tract's visual identity.

Between 1979 and 1986 we became professional neighbours, occupying the Bakery in Hawthorn, a recycled studio/office complex in inner Melbourne. In the early 1980s at the height of the postmodern era, Tract relocated to Lennox Street, Richmond, and to signal this new era of practice, I designed a new visual identity – which I revised again in the 1990s.

Over time, our professional activities have merged on projects where urban design and landscape architecture coexist with environmental graphics, and sense of place and identity occupy the same space.

We developed a strong friendship out of mutual professional respect, our passion for design and a need to feed off a different way of thinking. Perhaps the catalyst in this relationship was an approach I made to Steve, asking if I might sit in a corner of their studio to observe and learn. On many projects since then, we have brought together an unconventional conjunction of skills, since traditionally urban designers work at macro scale in three dimensions, whereas graphic designers work at micro scale in two dimensions.

What we've discovered is that surprisingly positive collaborations are often the outcome of different ways of thinking rather than like-minded thinking.

My interests as a graphic designer have been focused on aspects of design that fall between the disciplines of landscape architecture, urban design, architecture, industrial design, environmental graphic design, marketing communications, art, identity. I am happiest working with holistic design thinking that incorporates two-, three- and four-dimensional environments and engages with the public domain. Working with Tract, I've been immersed in various design disciplines involving time and motion, sensory and spatial experiences, micro and macro scales, exterior and interior environments, natural and built elements, always in ways that can go beyond the rational and raise the human spirit.

I am aware that this objective to raise the human spirit is inherent in Tract's design approach; and our collaborations often commence with a degree of humour and playfulness as a way of delving into an issue and working towards a design solution. The lighting tower we jointly designed for the NewQuay residential development in Melbourne's Docklands resembles an alien urban object, but we believe it successfully goes beyond the obvious practical design solution and expresses the energy and boldness of its surroundings. To make the tower, we engaged the skills of sheet metal magician, Robert Hook, who fabricates the sculptures of many prominent artists.

In another collaborative urban project, Pentridge Piazza, we were confronted as landscape architect and graphic designer with the site's somewhat chilling history as a gaol, and by the sombre thick walls of bluestone. In transforming this intimidating place into an attractive village environment, Rodney has made the public spaces spare and uncluttered, modern and ordered. Our task was wayfinding and signage. We designed an unconventional sculptural series of coloured objects: a modular system consisting of four metal shapes that are combined in various configurations to form asymmetrical objects that can be used as signage, seating, interpretive information displays and decoration. These objects wrap around corners; they are located in sinuous lines to link the core spaces; they curve around the planting. They act as 'follies' or sculptural pieces; they are place-making devices, enhancing orientation. They are a foil to the formality of the landscaping and help to add an independent, contemporary spirit to the historical site.

Garry Emery_A Collaborator's Perspective

It is very important as a designer to have the opportunity to extend a brief beyond a practical list of functions. And for me, the joy of working with Tract has always been the preparedness to play as designers and to think laterally, and the enthusiasm they display for the spirited design statement.

Garry Emery is a graphic designer. With no formal education, he has progressed from ticket writing to a leading international design practitioner, an achievement acknowledged by an honorary doctorate from RMIT University. Today he is a principal of Emery Frost, a Melbourne and Sydney based studio operating across Australia, Asia and the UK, developing corporate and brand identity, corporate communications, motion graphics, exhibitions and environmental graphic design from the scale of buildings to cities. For his contribution to architecture and urbanism he received the Presidents Award from Royal Australian Institute of Architects. He is a member of the prestigious Alliance Graphique Internationale. He is an Adjunct Professor at Deakin and RMIT Universities, and lectures internationally. His work has been widely exhibited, published and awarded.

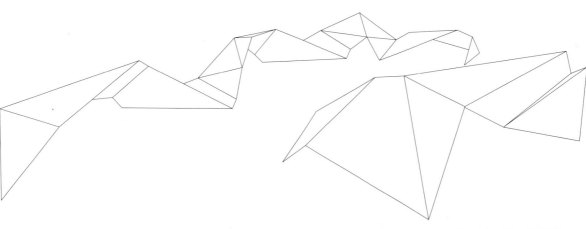

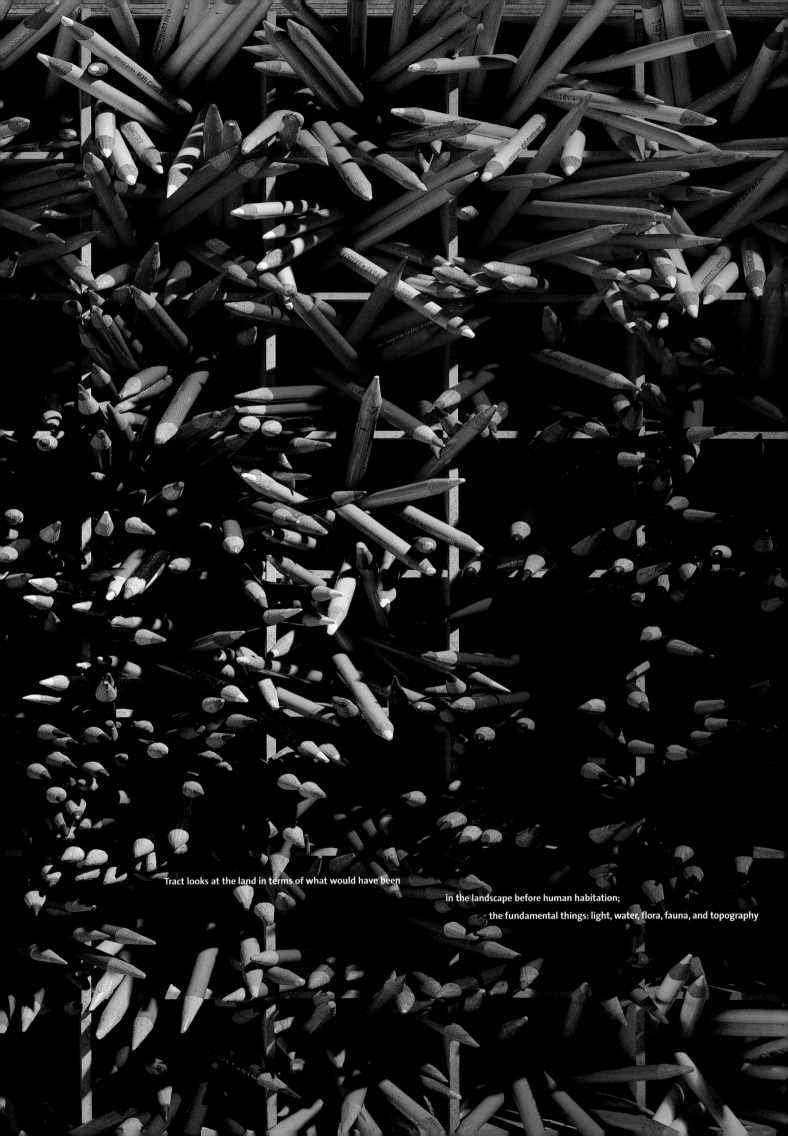

Tract looks at the land in terms of what would have been in the landscape before human habitation; the fundamental things: light, water, flora, fauna, and topography

Planning and design draw on people's collective experiences and memories, manipulating topography, planting, paving, axes, and patterns to reinforce sense of place,

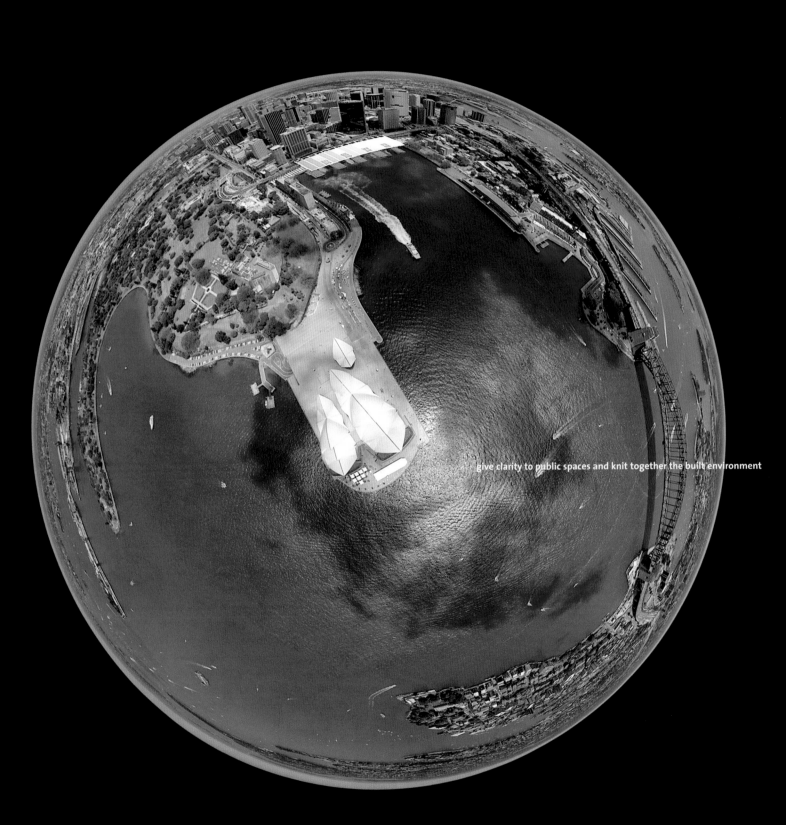

give clarity to public spaces and knit together the built environment

mplicated landscape designs relying on allusions   and overlays of meaning are more likely to lose their identity and gradually fall apart,

like chalk paintings on a pavement, than will a landscape design

based on an armature of strong, simple ideas able to endure through decades

Landscape has the capacity to endow local identity

through image-making overlaid with local ecology and culture

landscape architecture

in the utilitarian
responsibility to invest
the environment,
with an ordering idea
and transcending
utilitarian purposes

is grounded (literally)
and yet has the

at every scale,
charged with meaning
the fulfilment of
alone

Landscape architecture is comparatively young as a profession, only a hundred years or so. However, the genesis of contemporary landscape practice can be traced far back in time and place – to ancient markings of the land, to Asian and European garden traditions, to modern developments in the twentieth century. Yet despite the richness of many provenances, and the confidence with which landscape architecture was launched as a new academic discipline at the turn of the twentieth century, the profession a century later still finds difficulty in projecting a strong identity for itself.

Why should this be?

Contemporary landscape architectural practice is relegated behind architecture and urban planning. Too often it is dismissed simply as a decorative or environmental overlay useful for ameliorating the negative impacts of infrastructure, instead of being recognised as the professional discipline fundamental to the ordering and planning of the land.

Landscape architecture once held this broad role, but long ago it relinquished town planning and thus ceased to be central to regionally scaled planning operations. Today its place in the design of the environment is often misunderstood and undervalued; and apart from the few high-profile names in landscape architecture, the typical practitioner struggles to gain a clearly acknowledged position in planning and design.

What do landscape architects do? They plan and design the environment, from gardens to the scale of urban and regional planning. But architects and urban planners also work in these same areas, and misunderstandings arise concerning overlapping responsibilities of the three disciplines that were once integrated and indivisible.

Despite problems of overlapping professional responsibilities, one elemental aim differentiates the objectives that drive landscape architects and architects from the concerns and intentions that motivate urban planners. That elemental aim is design. By definition, planners do not design. Their vision is broadscale: to allocate functions to territories and zones, to assess projected growth and transportation patterns and assign them space on the map, maximising the availability of infrastructure and taking account of natural resources and terrain.

In contrast, the purpose behind design is to raise programme and functionality to an aesthetic, representational level. Order alone does not endeavour to achieve this: in themselves, the rational, utilitarian and statutory ordering operations of planning – zoning, infrastructure and circulation – are not concerned with design as a culturally representational or meaningful activity.

In practice, design differs in terms of its intent from the ordering operations of planning. We can easily understand the distinctions. Take a line of telegraph poles along a country road: whether or not the line of poles looks picturesque against the fields and distant hills, it exists primarily as a sequence of functional objects in the landscape.

It might perhaps serve as the subject of artists and photographers, but its coming-into-being is the result of a utilitarian planning decision to deliver electricity or telephony. In contrast, another set of poles in the landscape is readily recognised as art: Walter de Maria's Lightning Field in the desert of New Mexico (a grid of slender shiny metal poles) owes its significance both to its stark ordering presence, visually altering dramatically throughout the day, and to the generative concept that gives transcendent meaning to its coming-into-being. Between these opposite poles, as it were – visible ordering in the cause of (planning) functionality, and the ordering that results from the impulse to create a (useless) art object charged with significance – we find design, which is concerned with the application of aesthetic order and expression to practical tasks and objects.

Design is the territory of the landscape architect, who is grounded (literally) in the utilitarian and yet has the responsibility to invest the environment, at every scale, with an ordering idea charged with meaning and transcending the fulfilment of utilitarian purposes alone.

1.0

A holistic discipline fragmented

We might consider various sources as the 'origins' of modern landscape architecture – an obvious one being the grand estates of classical and baroque architects such as Vignola or Vanbrugh – but the immediate practical origins of the contemporary profession date from the mid-nineteenth century in the United States and Britain. Landscape architecture, as it emerged in the United States in the latter nineteenth century, developed from what Frederick Law Olmsted termed 'land planning'. This united agriculture, botany, meteorology, geology, geography, ecology, civil engineering, town planning, fine arts and history into a new professional discipline based on ideals of civic, social and environmental betterment. At the beginning of the twentieth century, formal university courses were offered first at Harvard and then at Columbia University.

The new discipline of landscape architecture was forged under pressure of many strands of thought. From initially being associated with the romantic and picturesque movements deriving from the European, and especially English, garden traditions, landscape architecture in America during the early twentieth century developed towards practice as an applied science concerned with the rational planning of the towns and new suburbs springing up in the path of the railway. It was also concerned with forest botany and preservation, the designation of large-scale wilderness areas, and study of the complex ecology of plant forms and their environments. Under the guidance of Olmsted, landscape architecture in the United States was also invested with strong social objectives, incorporating sympathetic observation of the ways people habitually use places, as well as the conviction that nature/landscape offers aesthetic, health-giving, spiritual, and other wholesome benefits to society, and can act to leaven by degrees the harmful conditions associated with urban living.

From 1900, landscape architecture at Harvard was taught alongside architecture (established as a course at Harvard only five years earlier). By 1910, landscape architecture in the United States was a profession in its own right. However, city planning – initially integrated with landscape architecture – was by then also clamouring for its own identity in the academy, and in the early 1920s it split to form a new discipline. This severed the holistic design nexus that had operated implicitly in the ordering of the inhabited environment to bind social, functional, urban, ecological and aesthetic needs. The split curtailed the power and integrity of both landscape architecture and urban planning throughout the twentieth century.

Ideal urban visions

During the nineteenth century, many cultural and social continuities of long standing were disrupted in Europe, Asia and North America, with large shifts of population taking place within countries as well as across frontiers and oceans. In Europe, rural folk abandoned the land for the growing industrial towns and cities, seeking employment and a better life. Millions, dislocated by poverty and persecution, immigrated to the United States where they crammed into cities before progressively dispersing west across the continent, dislodging the native inhabitants on the way. The railway, a forcible agent of change, tracked across formerly remote parts of the map, bringing innovation and uncertainty along with people, goods and communications. In both Europe and North America, the old order of stability and tradition was being shunted aside by new social, moral and economic paradigms and an unprecedented acceleration in the rate of progress and change.

These changes also affected the young nation of Australia, where the impacts of immigration and consequent displacement of native peoples were occurring in parallel with events in the United States. Australia's new population and its governmental, legal and cultural systems were drawn from Great Britain. But from the start Australia also absorbed ideas and inspiration from the United States, and during the twentieth century would gradually shift more towards American cultural values.

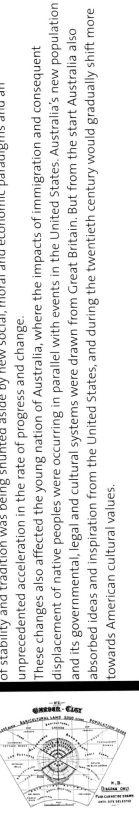

Garden City 1898

Two eminent nineteenth-century pioneers of landscape architecture, Frederick Law Olmsted in the United States and Ebenezer Howard in Britain, each proposed rational yet romantic city planning models for the new demographic conditions developing in their countries as a result of industrialisation, migration and mechanised mobility.

Olmsted and Howard separately conceived of small, bountiful and self-sufficient communities spread across the land. Olmsted's agrarian vision encompassed the nation as a single unit of design. This was 'land planning' stretching to its broadest reach. In the 1930s, the architect Frank Lloyd Wright also took a nationwide scope for his own Broadacre City, an idealistic concept for inhabiting the land without destroying the landscape, allocating an acre for every individual and grouping houses to preserve ample space for both cultivation and the retention of forests and prairies. Made possible by the motor car, the aeroplane and the telephone – agents of modernity that shrank distance and time – Broadacre City would (ideally) carpet the United States.

In Britain, Ebenezer Howard's idealistic Garden City vision of the late nineteenth century prefigured the construction of actual new towns in England early in the twentieth century. The Garden City was a diagrammatic urban blueprint: its concentric rings of central parkland, avenues, houses and gardens rippled outwards to precincts of factories, workshops, brickfields, and beyond them to allotments, orchards, asylums, convalescent homes, forests, and ultimately the large farms. The self-contained, mini city-state – with its balance of urban, rural and industrial functions – was connected to the distant capital and to other provincial centres by the railway.

In Britain and elsewhere, this essentially romantic town planning model prevailed until the post-World War II era, when cities exploded in scale and suburban development spread over the countryside. Increasing car ownership was a major factor in new urban development.

The myth that the urban/agrarian dream of self-sufficiency could accommodate exponential population growth became too obvious to ignore. By the 1960s, there was no longer any attempt to develop urban settlements that contained a balanced social, economic and cultural life. Instead, proliferating dormitory suburbs consumed land and marooned wives and children, along with those ill, retired or without work, in physical and social isolation. Sprawling development required extended road and transport networks predicated on the profligate consumption of energy, and ensuring communities were (and still are) bled of life as they emptied every morning.

Reforging old alliances

Landscape architecture in the early twentieth century – when still guided by the idealistic legacies of Olmsted and Howard – possessed an encompassing social and urban vision for managing the large-scale impact of human occupation on the land. This was achieved well before architecture began to hypothesise projects with social vision at such large scale, and before urban planning was even a profession in its own right. Such an integrated vision of the environment has been absent from most development for almost a hundred years. What has happened in this period to eclipse landscape architecture's leadership in the design of the greater environment?

A defining feature of the twentieth century was the explosion in global population. In the post-World War II era, cities burst traditional bounds and melded into spreading conurbations. (This continues relentlessly.) However, in the effort to cope with escalating population growth and unprecedented urban expansion, planners narrowed the scope of their operations to focus on an essential, pragmatic requirement: infrastructure provision. The result at a mass scale is that transport and communications networks, road layouts, street lighting, and sewerage would assume greater significance in determining the location, form and identity of new towns and suburbs than the interaction of topographical, environmental, climatic, contextual, cultural, social and aesthetic imperatives.

Specialisation and the functionalist determinants of urban planning have (perhaps necessarily) placed little value on the holistic design principles that earlier informed urban and landscape design: working with the topography and climate, balancing the interaction of built form and organic elements, using vernacular construction methods and materials, facilitating complex, interwoven cultural, social and economic relationships. Instead, new towns and suburbs everywhere would conform to the same simplistic but highly deterministic infrastructure specifications and mass market forces – trading spirit of place for blandness – and they have turned out all looking much the same: ubiquitous and anonymous.

Around the 1930s, landscape architects, trained to think at the scale of city and country, yielded their role in urban design to the new profession of town planning; in a failure of nerve they retreated largely into garden making. Architects too, once urban visionaries, by the mid-twentieth century were relinquishing their design leadership in town planning. Planners and engineers now took control of the built environment; and buildings and towns assumed the rational character of the instrumental planning decisions that determined their placement and form.

By the twenty-first century, the design of the environment – whether urban, rural or wilderness – has reached a pivotal point. Future development, if it continues as it has in the past, will compound the destruction of authentic communities and places. Any alternative development paradigm, however, requires new professional tactics and alliances capable of tackling the problems of urban blight, moribund towns, and threatened environments. The evidence of crisis is daunting: outreaching suburban tentacles demanding expensive infrastructure and services and extended commuting, the obliteration of distinctive urban identities, diminishing access to open space, limited availability of land for building, pressure on farming land and wildlife habitats, increasing air pollution, fouled waterways and debased wildernesses – all leading to the impossibility of sustaining living standards without drastic changes to how resources are allocated, consumed and recycled.

This throws out an overwhelming challenge that neither urban planners nor landscape architects by themselves are equipped to tackle. The scale and complexity of infrastructure requirements, and the extent of the social, technical, economic, cultural and ecological imperatives facing all future development, demand different, design-driven planning strategies that modern planners have not been expected, nor are able, to deliver. Similarly, architects and landscape architects working in isolation from planning processes are powerless to contribute to the design of the environment at the scale of districts, cities and provinces. The problems associated with urban density, alienation, placelessness, remediation, and resources are so compelling that only integrated strategies that reunite planning and design have any chance of addressing them adequately.

Design at the overall urban and environmental scale is territory that landscape architects and architects abandoned in the twentieth century. But in the twenty-first century, the need for ecological sustainability is driving the rehabilitation of old professional partnerships, harnessing the benefits of their combined synergy, to undertake the holistic planning and design of the environment.

Central Park, New York 1868

Frederick Law Olmsted

the story of tract

bonding of landscape
has made it possible
to operate beyond
expected of the
and to contribute to
environmental

Tract's professional team
architects and planners
for the practice
the usual scope
landscape consultant,
large-scale, complex
and urban projects

Tract's professional team bonding of landscape architects and planners has made it possible for the practice to operate beyond the usual scope expected of the landscape consultant, and to contribute to large-scale, complex environmental and urban projects.

Tract Consultants was established in Melbourne in 1973 with the objective of creating a new kind of planning and landscape consultancy. Tract was the offshoot of Merchant Builders, an enlightened design-and-build company whose partners David Yencken and John Ridge pioneered medium-density and cluster title residential developments in Victoria. At the time there were few landscape architects practising in Australia and most, however talented, had little formal training as there were barely any courses of landscape studies available.

The 1970s was a period of surging population growth and accelerating urban development, and as a result there was a major issue to tackle: large-scale landscaping and urban design operations. Australia urgently needed new design practices capable of envisaging appropriate responses to urban and suburban development that took account of the Australian landscape, climate and culture. So the time was ripe to start a practice combining urban planning/design and landscape planning/design, to set it up around a group of professionally trained young planners and designers, and to develop new directions for Australian landscape and urban design. Howard McCorkell was the first of the newly formed Tract group. Having completed architecture and planning degrees at the University of Melbourne, he travelled to Europe for three years between 1969 and 1972 before joining Tract. Rodney Wulff went overseas to study landscape architecture. After gaining a Bachelor of Landscape Architecture from the University of Oregon, a Master of Landscape Architecture from Harvard, and a PhD in Natural Resources Conservation from Cornell, he returned to Australia to join Tract in 1974.

Steve Calhoun, who grew up in the United States, completed a Bachelor of Landscape Architecture degree at Iowa State University, and a Master of Landscape Architecture at Harvard. He worked for Sasaki Walker initially, before deciding to leave California and join Tract in 1976.

Howard McCorkell, Rodney Wulff and Steve Calhoun brought together a combination of skills and experience that was unparalleled in urban design and landscape offices in Australia at the time. Tract quickly established itself, and in 1979 dissolved formal ties with Merchant Builders, although it continued to work closely with the group. George Gallagher, trained as both an engineer and a landscape architect, joined Tract in 1979. Mike Stokes, an architect with a strong background in urban design and sculpture, came into the practice in 1984.

As the first independent professional landscape practice in Australia – uniting skills in urban planning and design, natural resource planning, satellite imagery, computer modelling, and site planning and design – Tract was able to undertake large-scale masterplanning projects.

2.0

Vermont Park 1976

The earliest projects included a plan for Modbury-Golden Grove in Adelaide, an area expected to accommodate a quarter of the city's future growth (1974–1977); design guidelines for the Loddon Campaspe region in Victoria (1977), for the south-west coast of Victoria (1977), and for Vermont Park in Nunawading, Victoria (1976–1980), the latter a pioneering residential cluster design that received an Australian Institute of Landscape Architects award, and contributed to Merchant Builders being awarded the inaugural Robin Boyd Environmental Medal, 'for changing the face of residential Melbourne'.

Early on, Tract undertook significant urban design work. The redesign of the St Kilda foreshore (1977) set in train the full refurbishment of Melbourne's inner-city bayside, a project that continues almost thirty years on. Tract also designed many individual gardens, which led to larger residential projects including Kooralbyn Valley (Queensland, 1981–1983) and The Grange at Waitara in Sydney (1981–1983).

In 1981 Tract won the national competition for the redevelopment of the Newcastle Harbour foreshore. This pioneering urban regeneration commission established the reputation of the practice nationally. From Newcastle flowed other urban design and renewal projects around Australia, including the masterplan for the Queensland Government precinct in Brisbane.

Tract also involved itself in the development of the profession through teaching. Rodney Wulff and Steve Calhoun ran the Graduate Diploma in Landscape Architecture at RMIT from 1976 to 1981. Tract initiated a summer school in the early 1980s for landscape students around Australia, including mature students such as farmers and others intimately involved in stewardship of the land.

Tract directors throughout Australia have played a major role in the evolution of the firm. Rodney Wulff, Steve Calhoun, George Gallagher and Mike Stokes remain as key directors. Tract established additional offices, in Sydney in 1988 and Brisbane in 1990, and now in the early 2000s, the practice has grown and employs around sixty people. Stuart Pullyblank, an insightful landscape architect with considerable design skills in site planning and urban design and an extraordinary horticultural talent, had been with Tract since 1981. In 1992 Stuart was the founding director of Tract (WA) Pty Ltd and continues to collaborate with the various Tract offices throughout Australia. In Sydney, George Gallagher, along with Julie Lee, a highly skilled and talented designer who joined in 1989, have been the directors in charge of establishing the Sydney practice.

Stephen White, the founding Brisbane director, joined in 1994, and was a critical member of Brisbane's new office, bringing the highest quality in design and documentation in landscape architectural projects and office management. Stephen was joined in 2001 by Mark Doonar. With his vast experience in masterplanning, strategic and statutory planning, Mark brought a new skill level in planning and consultation to the Brisbane office and became a director in 2003.

Nevan Wadeson, the Melbourne planning director, joined the group in 1992. With his extensive experience and skill in major developments and strategic planning, Nevan has guided the Melbourne office to its current national prominence.

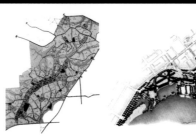
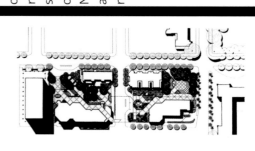

Modbury-Golden Grove 1977   St Kilda foreshore 1979   Queensland government precinct 1981

Integrating planning and

a single house on a block
the standard planning
Until the 1990s there
But changes in
demographics, family
and household structure
the redefinition of the

landscape architecture

has long been _____ paradigm in Australia. _____ was little alternative. _____ lifestyle choices, mobility, _____ have influenced _____ urban stereotype

Environments and communities have intrinsic values. Sound planning responds to a vision and springs out of functional thinking. It strikes a balance between sensitive readings of the territory and social values on the one hand, and the pragmatics of planning such as infrastructure and services, on the other.

As development sprawls further from established urban centres, transport, services and day-to-day interaction become more expensive. Communities are often isolated from established social, economic and cultural networks. Development has profound effects on the natural environment, particularly vegetation cover, water quality, and loss of biodiversity. Planning evaluates and ranks these issues; and masterplanning develops optimum design strategies for development.

Communities and local authorities increasingly realise the importance of achieving planning outcomes that deliver more than roads and utilities and zoning. In considering the long- and short-term impacts of development on the local environment as well as on a community's social and economic viability, sustainable development marshals the water cycle, manages waste, promotes energy efficiency and clean transport systems; it fosters the creation of safe, popular public spaces that engender social interaction, well-being and sense of community; and it recognises the need for local job creation and investment opportunities.

The old standard Australian planning model of a single house on a block was gradually redefined as the dominant suburban stereotype during the latter twentieth century, as Australian society experienced changes in lifestyle choices, mobility, demographics, and in family and household structure.

Cluster housing was a novel urban model when Merchant Builders pioneered it in Victoria in the 1960s, first at Elliston in Rosanna, then at Winter Park in High Street, Doncaster, and later at Vermont Park in Nunawading.

3.0

Tract Consultants was created as a division of the Merchant Builders group to provide consulting skills to land owners and agencies interested in the creative use of land resources and the quality of residential environments. In the early 1970s, the Victorian state government was persuaded by Merchant Builders projects such as Elliston and Winter Park to explore ways of enabling low- to medium-density cluster developments.

David Yencken was appointed by the government to chair the Cluster Titles Committee which produced the Cluster Titles legislation and the Model Cluster Code, a revolutionary model for the integrated subdivision of land and construction of houses.

These initiatives prefigured a more sweeping reappraisal of planning and subdivisional controls for residential development in the 1980s and 1990s, and contemporary controls based on site-responsive, performance-based planning criteria rather than traditional prescriptive regulations.

When Tract was established in the early 1970s, it was unheard of for landscape architecture and planning to be integrated in a single practice: Tract was the first organisation in Australia to combine these disciplines. Planning has been the key to enabling Tract to undertake large-scale regional and urban projects: to revitalise town centres, create new masterplanned communities (urban and rural), remediate degraded environments, and integrate the complex uses and services of modern landscapes and urban precincts. Early on, Tract implemented a landscape-based approach to strategic planning. In the late 1970s, the 500-hectare site in the Adelaide suburb of Modbury-Golden Grove was the first example of large-scale planning in Australia using the modern planning techniques pioneered by Tract. This approach was to analyse the landscape for key features, environmental values and logical pathways through the site, to identify areas of legible public domain, and to place the emphasis on creating a community rather than a subdivision.

The philosophy of integrating landscape and planning is perhaps most clearly demonstrated in Tract's seminal work for the Victorian Town and Country Planning Board in the late 1970s: regional guidelines to explain the benefits of site analysis and planning landscape-responsive developments. In a series of A4 and A3 broadsheets, Tract showed how to locate a house to best enjoy the site and maximise solar access, where to position driveways, septic tanks, and how to work with the land and care for it. The guidelines were a move away from the standard planning approach that disregarded topography, vegetation and soil types. Tract promoted environmental principles for planning subdivisions, working with the land, soils, wind, water and terrain.

These brochures are still used by many municipalities and planners today, either directly or as the basis for developing locally specific guidelines integrating current Environmentally Sustainable Development (ESD) principles. Since the early years, Tract's landscape design philosophy has been strongly driven by a site-responsive approach. There is a conscious endeavour to relate the landscape and architectural design to each site and to the local environment, drawing on Australian materials, vegetation, light and colours.

A foremost concern is that a sense of place needs to be created – or preserved – from the outset. In masterplanning, Tract looks at the land in terms of what would have been in the landscape before human habitation; the fundamental things: light, water, flora, fauna, and topographical features. Often the existing character of a place is ill-defined. Perhaps its only feature is a drainage line or a row of trees, but this becomes the basis on which to establish and amplify a sense of place that is distinctive and perhaps also has an aesthetic quality or order.

Yarra life and urban revitalisation, Melbourne, Victoria

3.1

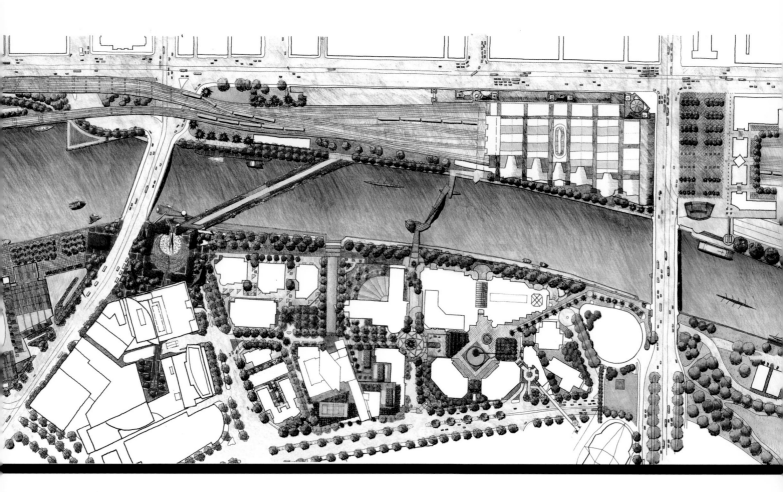

In the past, large stretches of Melbourne's Yarra River were relegated to industry. The latent urban potential of the south side of the river immediately across from the city began being realised in the 1980s. At that time, Tract was involved in planning and designing this area, renamed Southbank. Its incorporation into the life and identity of Melbourne has been spectacularly successful, and Tract continues to shape the evolution of the vibrant pedestrian and residential river precinct.

Location and aspect have much to do with Southbank's popularity. The southern riverbank not only catches the sun but also provides ideal north-facing views across the river to the CBD, at night seen glistening in the watery reflections. People flow back and forth across bridges from the city centre and mingle on the southern riverside or visit the adjacent arts precinct. Southgate's cafés, wine bars and shops ensure the riverbank is active day and night.

Typology is a strong generator of form in urban design. The edge of the river calls for a promenade. A typical Melbourne bluestone wall defines a promenade at water level, and there is also an upper, tree-lined walk beside the outdoor dining terraces where patrons sit and watch the passing parade.

Tract has produced urban design and planning guidelines for Flinders Wharf, a new residential area north of the river in what was formerly an underused industrial area.

Also, Tract is involved in the Yarra 2006 masterplan to coordinate the civic projects undertaken in preparation for the Commonwealth Games to be held in Melbourne in 2006.

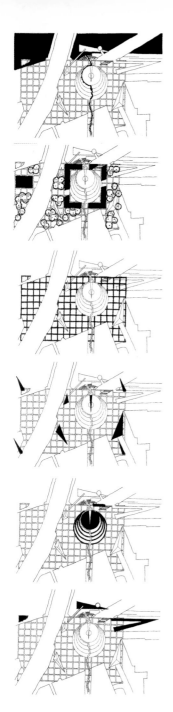

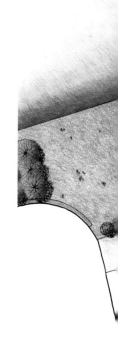

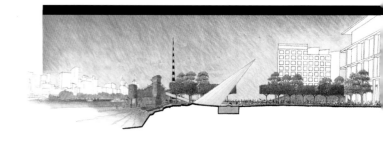

Yarra life and urban revitalisation, Melbourne, Victoria

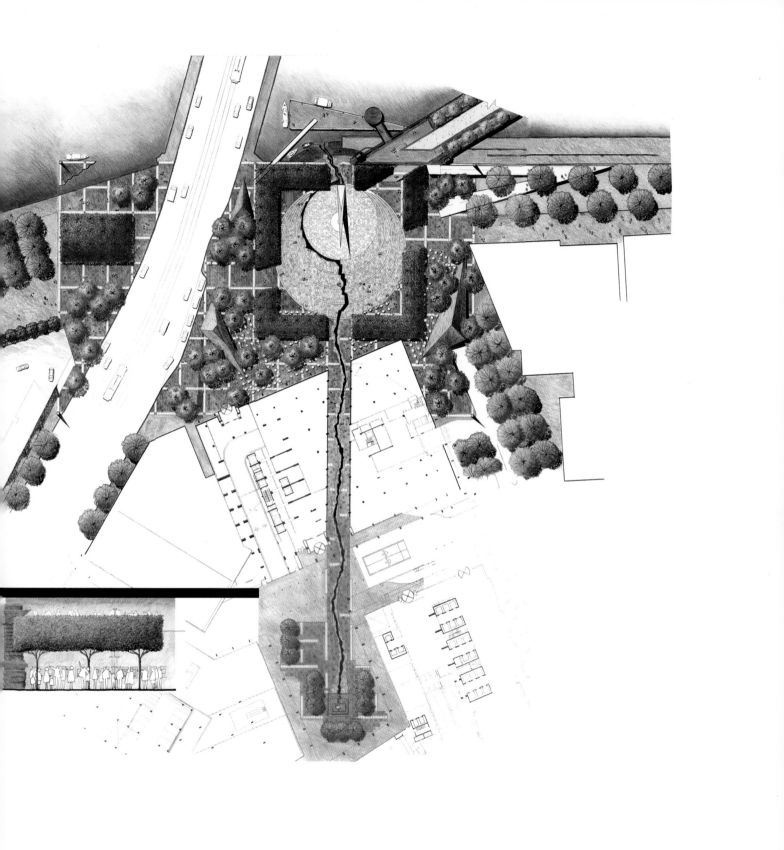

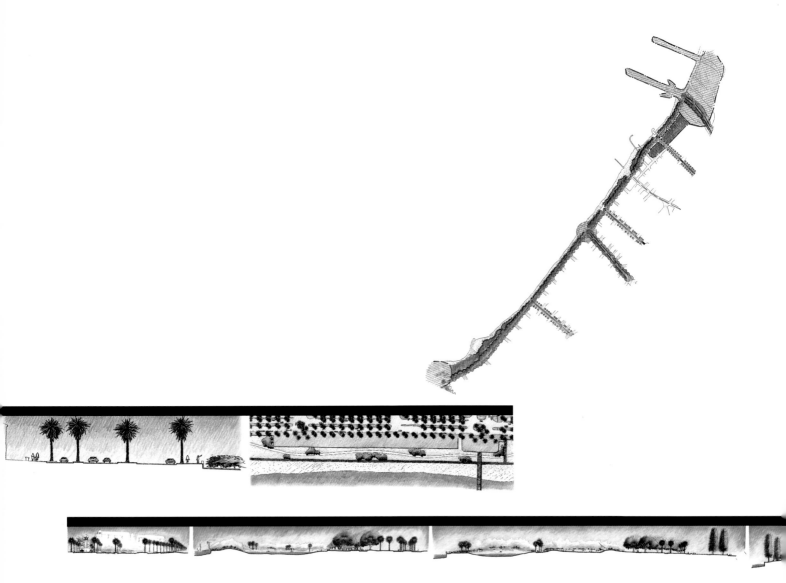

Bay Link and St Kilda foreshore, Melbourne, Victoria

3.2

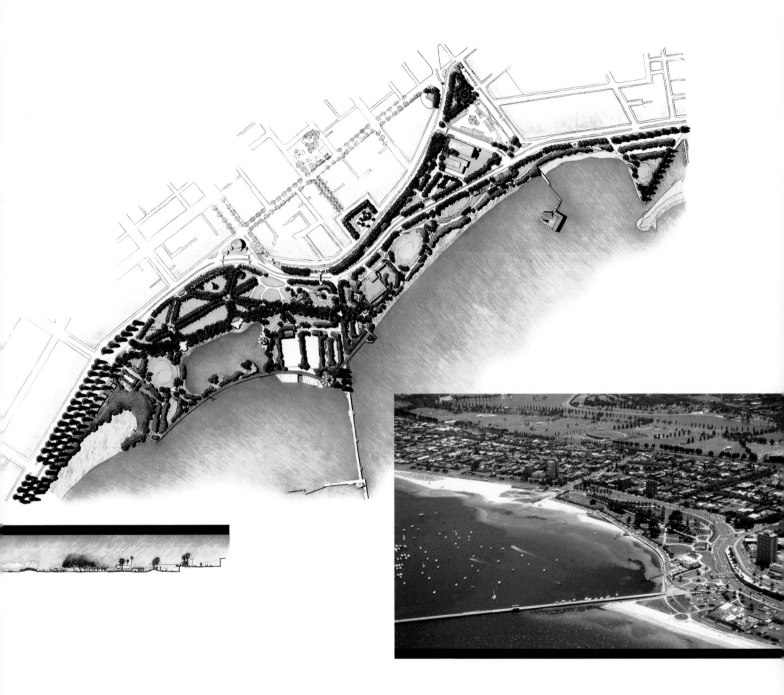

In the late 1970s, before its urban transformation, St Kilda was a rough, bleak bohemian enclave. Sand drifted onto the main road, dowdy boarding houses fronted the esplanade, and an air of seedy decay prevailed. There was no connection between central Melbourne and Port Phillip Bay, despite a nineteenth-century dream of city engineers to establish Melbourne as the Riviera of the southern hemisphere.

From 1977 to 1981, Tract undertook a study of the bay foreshore (from Cowderoy Street, the South Melbourne boundary, to Head Street, the Brighton boundary) and prepared a masterplan.

The impending upgrade to Beaconsfield Parade, the main road skirting the bay, was an opportunity to herald the water frontage and tie the bay precinct in with key roads leading back towards the city. Tract developed the public space typology for the crucial zone between the water's edge and Beaconsfield Parade. An inventory of possible uses for this area focused on access to the water. Consequently, the planning/design strategy is based on access to public space rather than on an aesthetic or thematic landscaping treatment.

A new bluestone seawall was built along the edge of the beach, and a network of green parklands was planted along the bay between the seawall and Beaconsfield Parade, down to Elwood Beach.

Existing small clusters of Canary Island palms at key nodal points in St Kilda were linked by hundreds of mature palms planted to form a sweeping line defining the bay and uniting the bayside suburbs. A widened pavement beside the seawall accommodates cyclists and skaters as well as pedestrians. Tract encouraged street activities and outdoor cafés and restaurants to bring life to the rejuvenated esplanade.

Coastal management, Victoria

3.3

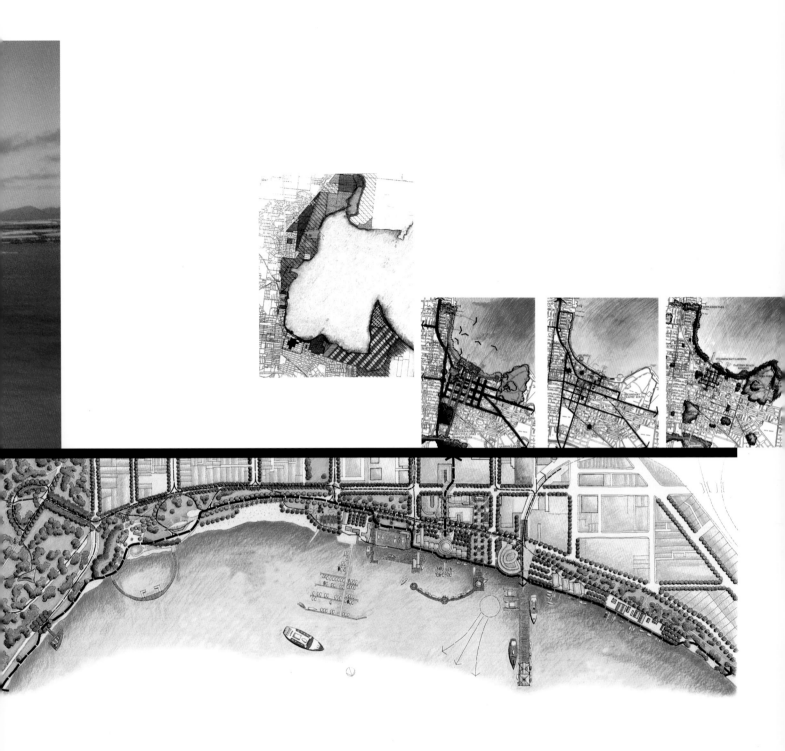

In the late 1970s there was growing interest in preserving the natural environment. Tract produced a natural heritage inventory that included scenic views. It was the first step in design guidelines giving greater significance to the quality of the natural environment rather than to individual lots.

Although directed from a design perspective, the guidelines represent a shift into planning, requiring the combined skills of planning and landscape architecture.

This study led in the early 1980s to Tract undertaking a series of landscape studies investigating the ecological, aesthetic and functional requirements of coastal land planning for Port Phillip Bay, the first such planning study in Australia. The data informed its strategic masterplanning.

Tract's coastal design and siting studies created a framework for planning and managing coastlines, taking account of genius loci as well as environmental and other site-sensitive issues. Physical analyses were augmented by community consultation, something new for such studies in Australia at the time.

In 1998 this work became the model for the *Siting and Design Guidelines* and *Landscape Setting Types for the Victorian Coast*. These documents are now incorporated into all coastal planning schemes in Victoria and are used on a daily basis by planning bodies in making design assessments along the coast.

Specific landscape-based planning projects followed, including the Corio Bay Foreshore Management Plan (1995), Corio Bay Coastal Action Plan (2003), City of Greater Geelong Study of Open Space Networks (2001), and the Portland Foreshore Masterplan (1995).

Tract produced an urban masterplan (1994–1997) for the provincial city of Geelong, south of Melbourne, which was built with its back to Corio Bay. The city wanted to benefit from embracing the waterfront and attracting tourists. Tract's masterplan turns Geelong's attention to the bay by establishing an axial connection along the town's other neglected waterfront, the Barwon River.

The curving waterfront of Corio Bay is integrated through a chain of landscape events that link leisure activities associated with the pier, restaurants, shops, museums, parks and promenades.

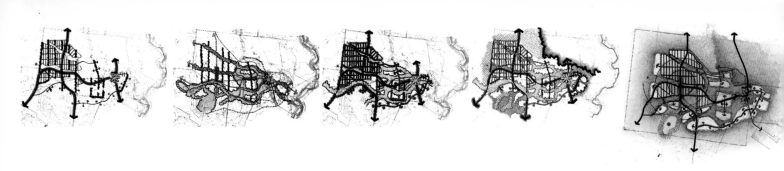

Eynesbury Station, Victoria

3·4

Eynesbury Station is a broad-acre rural holding 40 kilometres west of Melbourne between the growth areas of Werribee and Melton. It is the largest parcel of land in single ownership in this region. A portion of 1300 hectares has been rezoned for an integrated township and recreational development that incorporates environmentally sensitive design, farming and environmental initiatives.

The rural-style township (of approximately 3000 lots) includes retail, educational and recreational developments. There is a major golf course with clubhouse and business conference facilities (a second course is planned). Residential precincts incorporate a range of household types that generate a complex social mix.

Residents enjoy equestrian facilities and riding tracks, the landscape of native woodlands and grasslands, as well as the nearby historic homestead. Grey effluent water is recycled on the golf course and reticulated for agricultural use, and a new wetland drainage system helps protect the Werribee River.

Broadbeach Local Area Plan and masterplan, Gold Coast, Queensland

3·5

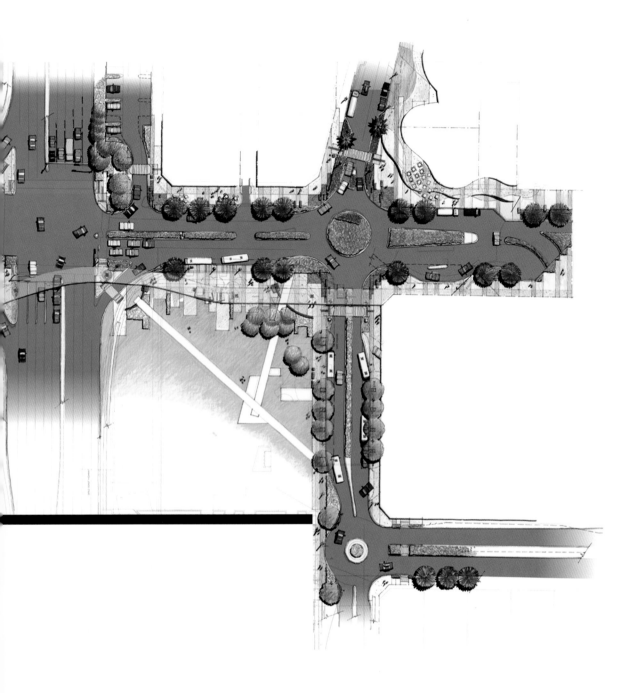

The Gold Coast City Council required a development catalyst to propel sleepy Broadbeach to become a significant destination in the future. The study area for the masterplan to achieve this included Jupiter's Casino, the Broadbeach Mall and Oasis Shopping Centre, Kurrawa Beach, Pacific Fair Shopping Centre and the Gold Coast Convention Centre, all symbols of the rampant development that has transformed the Gold Coast into Australia's Miami since the 1960s.

The masterplanning process brought together diverse interests. Stakeholder workshops gave residents, corporate organisations, community groups,

landowners and business owners the opportunity to come together and discuss issues. This consultation process reinforced concurrent work by Tract on the Local Area Plan, notably issues about pedestrian access and active public-private interfaces.

Public safety is an important neighbourhood issue. The two- and three-storey bed-sitters that line many of the streets generate the built character of the area. Given the vagaries of a largely transient population, these buildings provide a needed type of accommodation, contribute a human scale, and enable natural surveillance that high-rise buildings tend to prevent.

To provide the area with a distinctive identity and to help improve orientation in a flat terrain of undifferentiated suburban streets and strip commercial development, the masterplan envisages several three- to six-storey buildings being capped by distinctive roof-line elements to act as landmarks: the roof as billboard.

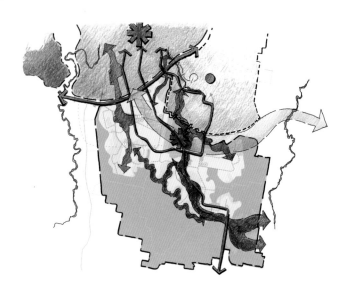

Ripley Valley Community Plan, Queensland

3.6

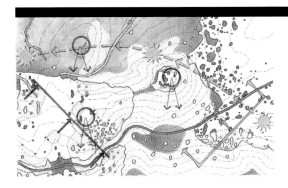

The Ripley Valley is one of the largest urban growth areas in fast-growing South-East Queensland. It is located just 4.5 kilometres from the established town of Ipswich, and extends for more than 100 square kilometres. It has been identified as suitable for development for housing up to 100,000 people over 25 years.

The Ripley Valley Community Plan provides a vision for this future and incorporates the local council's commitment to protecting the valley's special qualities. It presents objectives addressing issues of sustainable development and possible strategies for implementation.

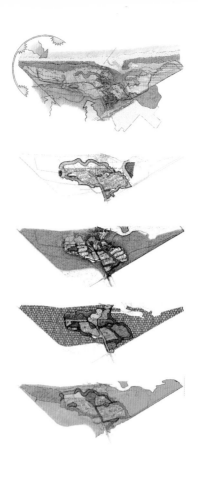

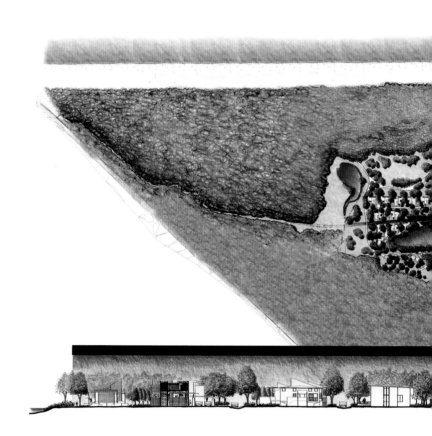

North Beach, Byron Bay, New South Wales

3·7

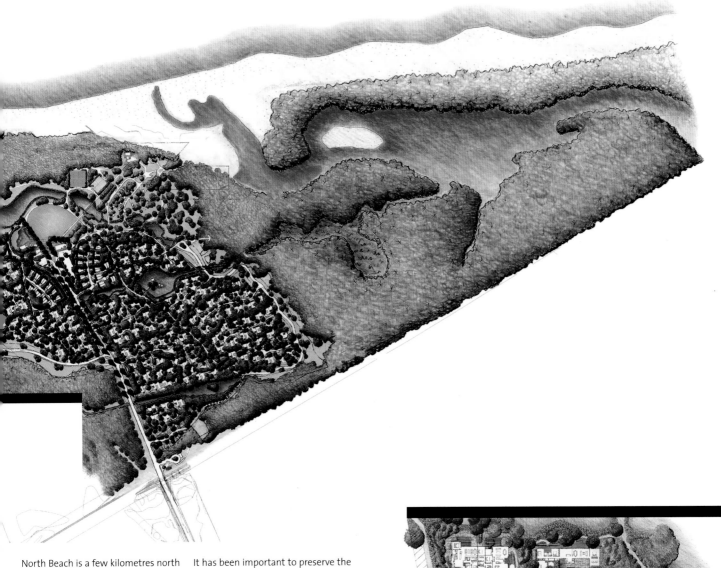

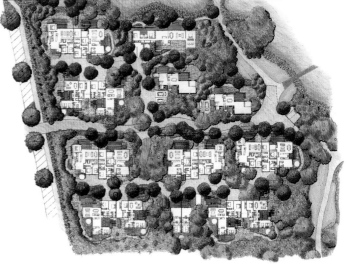

North Beach is a few kilometres north of the centre of Byron Bay, one of the great beach towns of the New South Wales north coast. The site area of approximately 88 hectares includes 2.5 kilometres of beach frontage. Parts of the site had been previously developed as a resort with a nine-hole golf course. On three sides the site is surrounded by sensitive natural environments: the Tyagarah Nature Reserve, Belongil Creek, and the coastal dunes.

Tract's masterplan envisages a tourism development with the character of a small seaside village, which is in keeping with the existing character of the site and its coastal context.

It has been important to preserve the setting of this small seaside village as a perpetual environmental reserve. The masterplan confines development to less than 25 per cent of the site, with the remainder to be revegetated with the plant communities that would have existed before the site was originally cleared.

Lynbrook Estate, Victoria

3.8

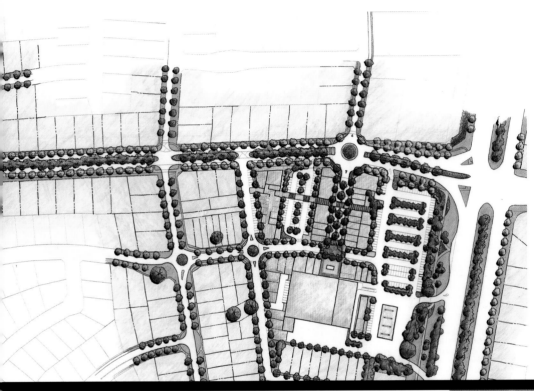

On casual observation, Lynbrook appears a typical suburban estate, but what lies beneath is a ground-breaking Water Sensitive Urban Design (WSUD) drainage and stormwater treatment system. Lynbrook is the first suburb to apply WSUD techniques in metropolitan Melbourne. Tract, as planner and urban designer for the project, introduced water management principles which include using green swales to enable natural surface infiltration to treat stormwater before it enters the lake. Concrete gutters and standard stormwater pits are unnecessary.

A new boulevard entry road from the highway gives long axial views to remnant trees and the wetland water treatment area. Tract relocated a linear parkland and water treatment system to the west of the site, near the rail line, creating a connected pedestrian, cycle and passive open space path along the whole length of the estate, buffering the elevated rail line.

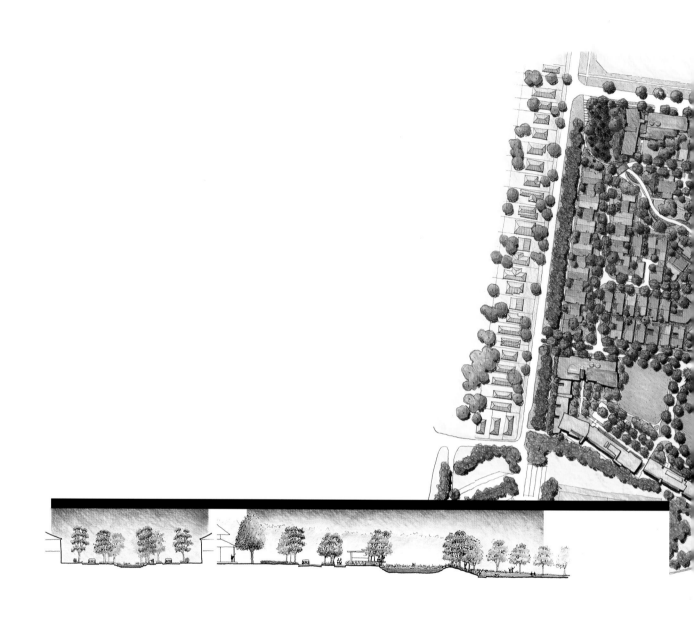

City signature and urban design projects_2006 Commonwealth Games Village, Royal Park, Victoria

3.9

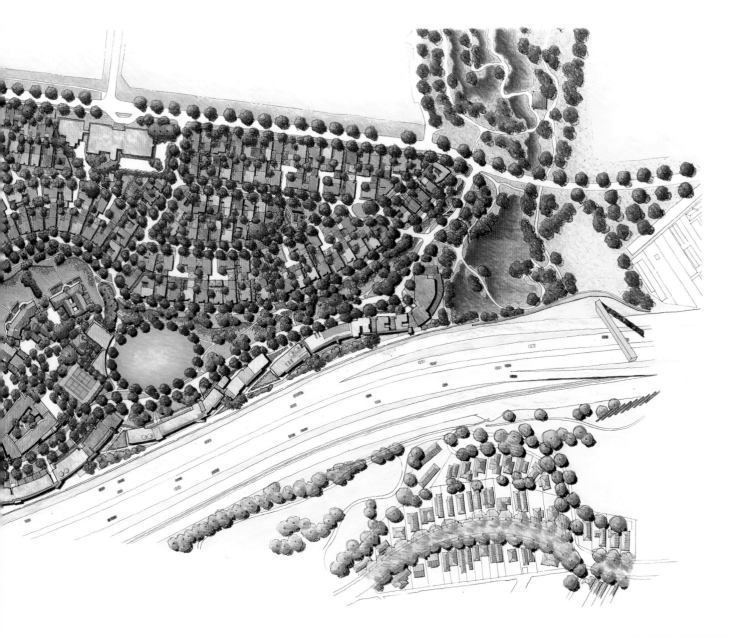

Tract, as masterplanner and landscape architect, played a key role in shaping the Village Park Consortium's successful bid to develop the 2006 Commonwealth Games Village in the Melbourne suburb of Parkville on behalf of the Victorian State Government. During the Games, the 20-hectare site will house 6000 athletes and officials and numerous games-related services. Post-Games, the Village will be converted to a residential neighbourhood of 1000 dwellings, including mixed-use and aged care precincts.

A formative element of the masterplan is the central corridor of open space. This allows a free flow of visual and physical connections through the site, from the central heritage precinct to Royal Park. Ecologically sustainable design principles inform the landscape design which incorporates advances in stormwater management, safeguards local flora and fauna biodiversity, and requires less irrigation and chemical control than conventional landscapes. It provides a beautiful natural setting.

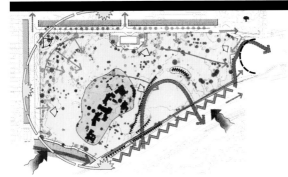

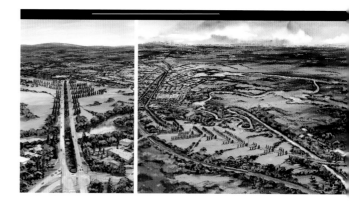

　　　　　Urban village, Strathpine, Queensland

3.10

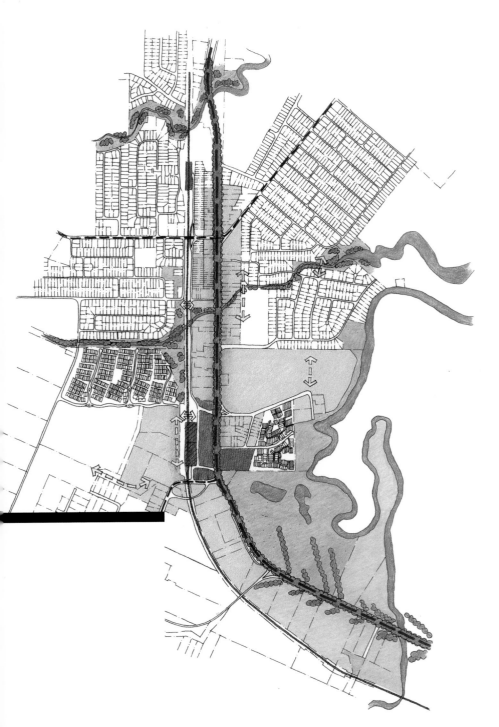

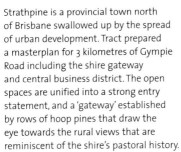

Strathpine is a provincial town north
of Brisbane swallowed up by the spread
of urban development. Tract prepared
a masterplan for 3 kilometres of Gympie
Road including the shire gateway
and central business district. The open
spaces are unified into a strong entry
statement, and a 'gateway' established
by rows of hoop pines that draw the
eye towards the rural views that are
reminiscent of the shire's pastoral history.

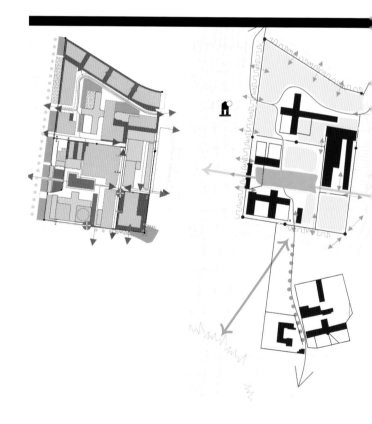

60_   Pentridge_Coburg Prison complex redevelopment, Coburg, Victoria

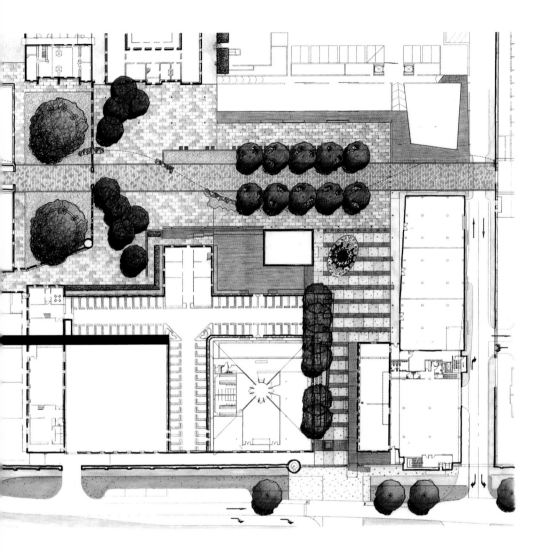

3.11

Pentridge is a name synonymous with incarceration and misery. Since the early nineteenth century, it was one of Melbourne's notorious prisons, a forbidding site ringed by thick stone walls. As planner, urban designer and landscape architect, Tract faced the challenge of removing the stigma and turning it into a desirable residential and mixed-use village. The main planning issues include incorporating the walled site back into the surrounding community, providing links to local transport networks, conservation of heritage elements, and preserving the natural features of the land.

Tract advises the two separate land-owners developing the complex, Pentridge Piazza Pty Ltd and Pentridge Village Pty Ltd.

Pentridge Village
The entire Pentridge site will eventually be developed with approximately 2000 dwellings and will include a variety of medium-density housing types (in existing and new buildings) and educational and entertainment facilities in some of the key historic structures. A new 1.2-hectare park is located in the centre of the new residential precinct, and will act as a link to the stormwater treatment facility at Merri Creek. The original gaol is part of this development, and historic places will be preserved (notably Ned Kelly's cell and burial place). The plan includes commercial and medium-density residential development as well as public lanes, plazas and meeting spaces.

Pentridge Piazza
Tract coordinated the design guidelines and masterplan, and generated the urban designs for all public areas. Important references to the site's past are preserved and incorporated into a high-quality commercial and residential development. The major objective is to revitalise the site and create diverse living and working opportunities close to public transport, community and commercial facilities.

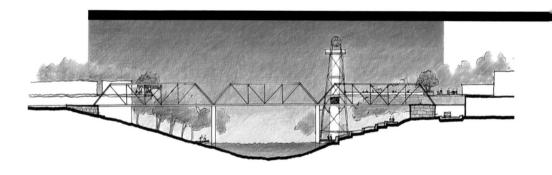

Ipswich River Heart project, Ipswich City Council, Queensland

3.12

Ipswich City Council commissioned
Tract to participate in a project to revitalise
the Ipswich Central Business District.
Ipswich, west of Brisbane, used to be
a wealthy coal-producing city, and retains
some vestiges of nineteenth-century
civic grandeur. But its heyday is long gone
and the city needs to rejuvenate its
urban fabric and its civic image. Five key
development principles are identified
to activate both the Top of Town and
the CBD reach of the Bremer River:
improve accessibility; ensure pedestrian
links are easy to identify and to use; locate
CBD destinations strategically; stage
infrastructure that does not rely on
the private sector; add value to potential
private developments.

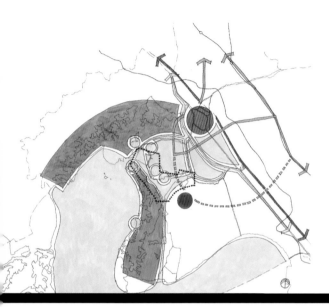

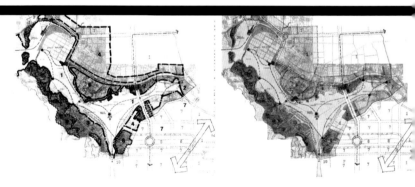

Regional and metropolitan projects_Wuli Lake, Wuxi City, China

3.13

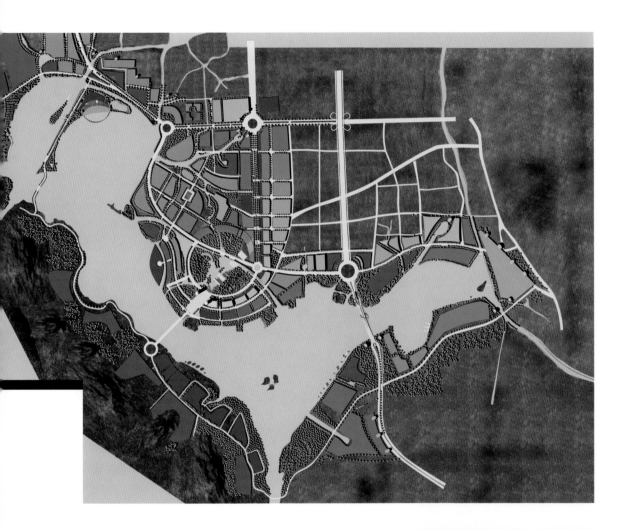

Wuxi is one of several cities in the Yangsi River delta, located at the northern end of Tai Hu, one of China's largest freshwater inland lakes. The city has existed for 3000 years. The area of the masterplan covers about 24 square kilometres around Wuli Lake. The masterplan draws heavily on the organic city form, balancing this against the need for a more formal, more efficient, more legible and modern planning approach.

The major functional areas (commercial, residential, open space) are differentiated, and the road network hierarchy designated by coordinated (but not regimented) main, secondary and local roads. The plan delineates generous areas of open space as well as the major squares and other smaller, but important, open spaces at strategic points.

Double Bay, Tai Hu, China

3.14

A study of this scenic 3.5-square-kilometre site in the Da Fu area of Jiangsu Province was undertaken to coordinate land uses, lay out public open spaces, produce a traffic plan, define controls for general building form, heights and layouts, and ensure sustainable development that encourages tourism, recreation and sight-seeing activities.

the new public park

metropolitan park

Central Park, designed in 1857

the quintessential _____ is still New York's

by Olmsted and Vaux

The Park and the Promenade

4.0

During the eighteenth and nineteenth centuries, large metropolitan parks were incorporated into the planning of cities. The parks were democratic, open to all, yet their models were the grand aristocratic estates and ancient royal hunting parks. Surrounded by urban development, these extensive public parks preserved a rustic memory in the city and provided opportunities for recreation and quiet meditative escape. The quintessential metropolitan park is still New York's Central Park, designed in 1857 by Olmsted and Vaux, which creates a lush foil to the gridded concrete canyons of the city, and clearly manifests the belief in nature's power to offer respite from the negative effects of urbanism and industrialisation.

Many of the worst aspects of the nineteenth-century industrial city – for which the metropolitan park offered such evident relief – were ameliorated in the twentieth century by cleaner industrial technologies and modern planning. Parks have become valued more for their ornamental qualities and civic prestige than as places in the city to retreat to in order to experience nature. Despite the increased density and pace of contemporary cities, urban citizens of today often have less urgent need than their nineteenth-century predecessors to seek out the virtual countryside of the metropolitan park, being as likely to set off in family cars for the actual countryside (or the beach) to find a direct experience of nature.

Yet demand for new parks continues. The problem is where to put them. In existing cities, urban consolidation means that few, if any, traditional public parks could again be planned at a grand metropolitan scale, and so most new city parks are confined to the scale of gardens tucked into interstitial and marginal remnants of land. The vestigial contemporary public park – like its forerunner, the traditional park – is still a place of refuge, but now it has become a haven from traffic rather than from the ugliness and grime of polluting industries. Where it recycles urban territory, the new public park often does approximate the scale of the traditional metropolitan park. The sites for modern large new parks tend to be linear: land reclaimed from disused rail lines, degraded industrial river banks, open stormwater culverts, abandoned wharves. These are tough, gritty places – the armpits of cities – and there is little bucolic about them or their insalubrious neighbourhoods.

For these new parks at the metropolitan scale, the defining model lies not in their capacity for the picturesque re-creation of nature or countryside – the central idea of the traditional public park – but in the principal activity that both traditional and contemporary types of park sustain: walking. The idea of the walk or promenade has always underpinned the design of urban parks. The promenade is an urban typology deriving from the age-old social ritual of people emerging from their homes in the evening to stroll, take the air, perhaps stop at a bar and watch the passing parade. Traditionally, the promenade has been the main agency of social conviviality in the public realm. Today that ritual is extended by the jogger and the skateboarder. Whether ritualised or not, promenading – jogging, cycling, skating – remains an agency for conviviality and recreation in contemporary urban societies.

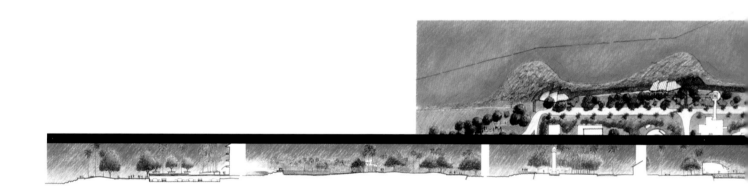

72_   Cairns Esplanade, Queensland

4.1

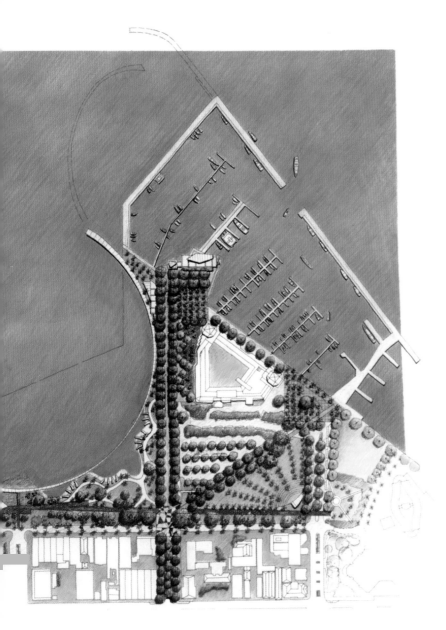

Cairns was a tropical coastal country town that has become an international tourist mecca. Many visitors are attracted by the tropical climate and the migrating birds that flock to the rich feeding grounds along the tidal flats of Trinity Inlet. When the tide retreats however, the muddy flats stretching for 800 metres present a disappointing image. A design competition was held in 1998 to overcome this problem without destroying the bird habitat, and to establish a safe swimming lagoon free of box jellyfish and crocodiles.

In the winning design by Tract and Cox Rayner Architects, a curved seawall at one end of the long esplanade creates a raised lagoon – functioning like a ha-ha – so that even when the tide is out there is water in the bay. Along the new boardwalk, 6 to 8 metres wide, people walk, jog, cycle, birdwatch or relax by the waterfront. Nodes from the boardwalk extend back into the town, helping to revitalise the town centre with new activities and direct visual links to the bay.

Cairns Esplanade, Queensland

Cairns Esplanade, Queensland

Cairns Esplanade, Queensland

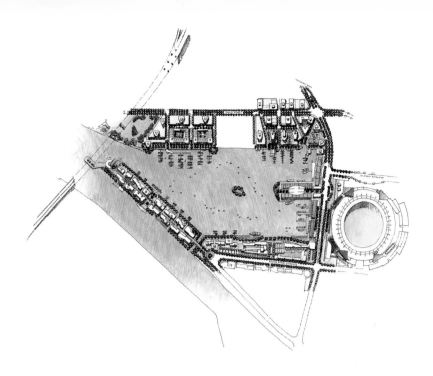

NewQuay, Docklands, Melbourne, Victoria

4.2

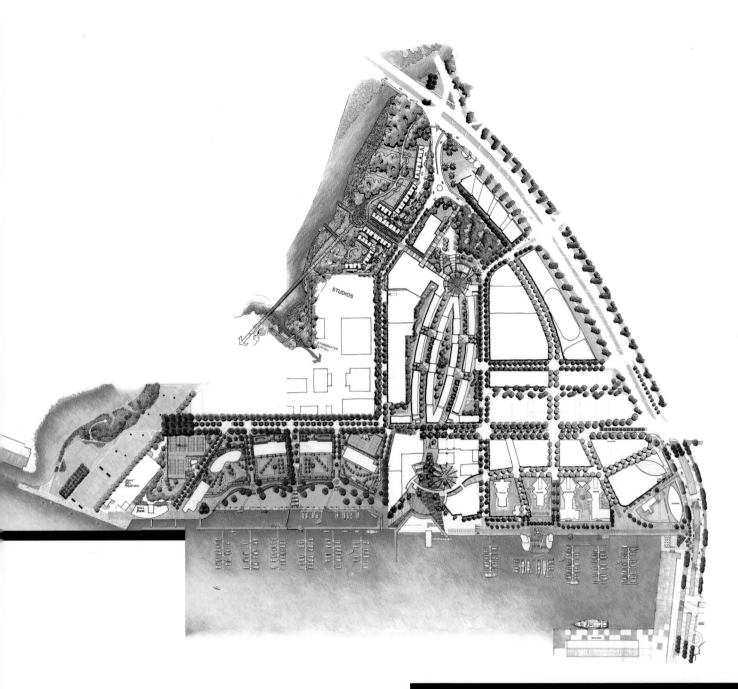

STUDIOS

Melbourne's vast new Docklands area, when finally all developed, will double the size of the existing CBD, which lies adjacent. The initial task is to create special places within this enormous former industrial precinct and attract residents, businesses and visitors to cross a railway line that divides Docklands from the city.

Newquay, the first major residential precinct development in Docklands, faced a daunting challenge. The completion of Stage One would remain surrounded by unsightly disused wharf and container hardstand. Yet it was critical that the precinct function as a major attraction from the outset. The public realm is conceived of as a high activity zone of restaurants, cafés, takeaways, bakeries, convenience stores and other retail outlets. Tract provides a discernible hierarchy of open spaces – waterfront promenades, plazas, intimately scaled laneways and major boulevards. Newquay quickly developed into a vibrant cosmopolitan precinct with a new Melbourne harbourside character incorporating contemporary sculpture, building art and follies.

NewQuay, Docklands, Melbourne, Victoria

Manly Interchange, Corso and ocean beach, Sydney, New South Wales

4.3

Manly Interchange, Corso and ocean beach, Sydney, New South Wales

4.3

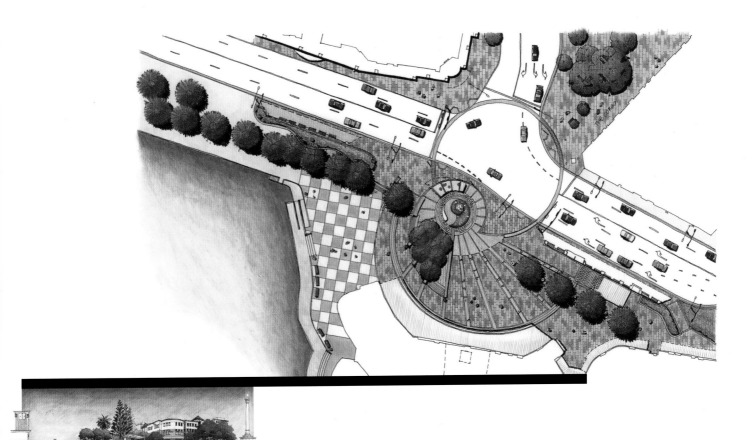

Manly is a popular traditional seaside suburb with frontages both to the harbour and the ocean. The Corso, running across a narrow strip of land, connects the harbourside wharf and bus interchange to the ocean beach. Tract's design for the new bus interchange rationalises and clarifies the formerly chaotic, intersecting pathways of buses and pedestrians and creates a safe, legible hub readily understood by residents and tourists.

From here the route to the beach is via the Corso. This well-worn pedestrian street, lined with shops and cafés, was shabby and cluttered. Tract's design for the Corso reorganises the public space and includes new lighting, street furniture, paving and planting. It was important to retain the existing urban

character; and the popularity of this much-visited outdoor public space required that a phased upgrading be undertaken to ensure that it was never entirely closed during works.

The ocean beach had also suffered from the constant parade of visitors. Tract upgraded the beach promenade, retaining its existing casual character. The new seawall and sets of steps onto the beach help protect the seafront and provide easy access and places to sit. The interventions are subtle and low-key, dictated by observation and analysis of the site.

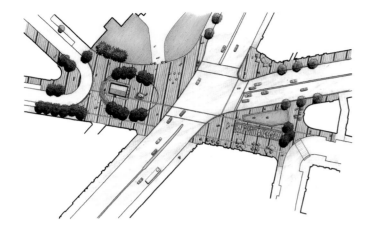

Taylor Square redevelopment, Darlinghurst, New South Wales

4.4

Taylor Square, like many urban places in Sydney, is the outcome of a pattern of land subdivision and existing roads. The square, which forms an eastern gateway into central Sydney, has two distinct identities. On the northern side of Oxford Street it is a civic precinct of major nineteenth-century institutions: the old gaol, the elegant Greek Revival court house, and a police station, all built of characteristic Sydney sandstone, and a large hospital. The southern side of Oxford Street is commercial, lively and sleazy. The square is notorious as the centre of the popular annual gay Mardi Gras parade, a Sydney institution.

Street closures following completion of the Eastern Distributor road system provided an opportunity to revitalise the badly scuffed and tatty Taylor Square as a landmark public space.

Granite paving provides a pictorial order to the vast area. Small intersecting modules are patterned into bands setting up a bold, dynamic composition.

The gay culture is acknowledged in the pink granite, triangle motif and steel cast studs on light poles, bins and stone seats (anti-skateboard devices).

Oxford Street lies above Sydney's second colonial water supply, Busby's Bore. The underground tunnel contains twenty-eight shafts sunk into the bore. Shaft No 5 is located at Taylor Square. This historical reference

is translated into a design feature: a fountain that provides the perpetual sound of running water. The fountain announces the new heart of Taylor Square and refreshes this high-use precinct. It is interactive and dynamic, with programmable shows that include fog and vertical and angled jets. Mature Angophora trees encircle the raised north terrace and establish an urban character that will further develop as they mature.

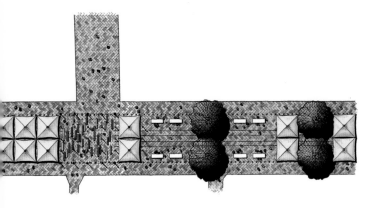

4·5

**Oxford Street Mall redevelopment,
Sydney, New South Wales**

Landscape architecture is often about changing negative perceptions of a place. The existing streetscape of this busy, lucrative but run-down inner-suburban mall projected a nondescript urban identity. The brief was to regenerate this central retail core of Bondi Junction, which is undergoing considerable change as the result of a $A1 billion retail redevelopment.

The Oxford Street Mall is also a major transport interchange for trains and buses. The railway station is the busiest non-central Sydney station in the metropolitan area. The main entry to the bus/rail interchange is in the centre of the mall, and 15,000 pedestrians daily pass between the railway station and the Eastgate shopping centre.

Oxford Street curves gently to follow the contours in the landform. A result of this curving is that the mall feels spatially contained, since from the centre there is no direct view east or west to either end.

The linear placement of furniture, street trees and the catenary lighting define the space of the mall as a 'street'. The design language is contemporary, and uses high-quality materials and finishes.

Effective wayfinding is important both for orientation and safety, especially in a public complex of this scale. The broad, uncluttered spaces enable easy visual and pedestrian access and draw people safely into the heart of the mall. There is ample space for events and celebrations and entertainment. Removable market canopies allow flexibility.

The thematic design of the mall develops around the notions of transport. Old tram tracks from a bygone era are expressed down the centre of the mall. Tramway elements are also incorporated into the children's play area in the form of working levers and wheels.

Newcastle harbour foreshore, New South Wales

4.6

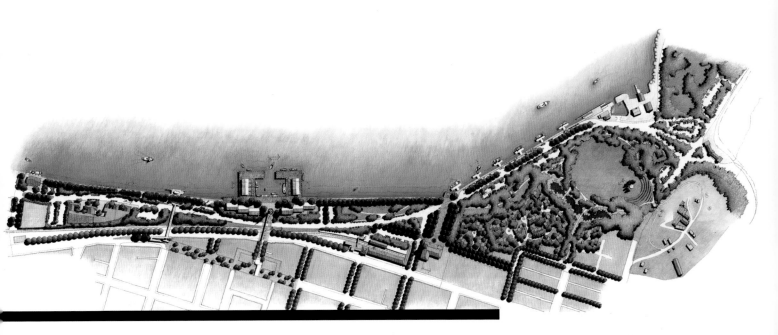

The first urban design competition in Australia was held in 1981. The subject was Newcastle, a regional coastal city to the north of Sydney. The declining industrial city was in an advanced state of physical and psychological decay; its infrastructure was rotting and the population suffering culturally and economically.

Tract by this time had completed work on the St Kilda esplanade, based on an idea of the Corniche to invigorate the neglected bayside waterfront of Melbourne. Tracts's winning design for Newcastle is based on bridging the physical barriers severing the town from its Hunter River waterfront – a steep hill, a major road and a rail line. The industrial genius loci is expressed in the retention of the existing street typology and in the new steel bridge (Newcastle was a major steel-producing centre) spanning the main road to join the town with the riverside park.

Newcastle had always turned away from its dirty waterfront and harbour, and a massive effort was required to clean up the derelict industrial foreshore. When the design of the park was implemented and local people could finally see the benefits of being down on the river, the area immediately became popular. Fishing jetties, observation decks, outdoor cafés, restaurants, and animated promenades lined with Norfolk Island pine trees entirely changed the spirit and culture of Newcastle; with the progressive consequences of renewed confidence and urban vitality, the city's fortunes have reversed.

For a building programme to achieve a comparable social and urban impact, the cost would be enormous.

Newcastle harbour foreshore, New South Wales

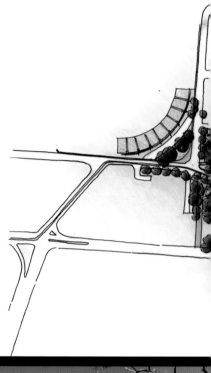

Claisebrook, East Perth, Western Australia

4.7

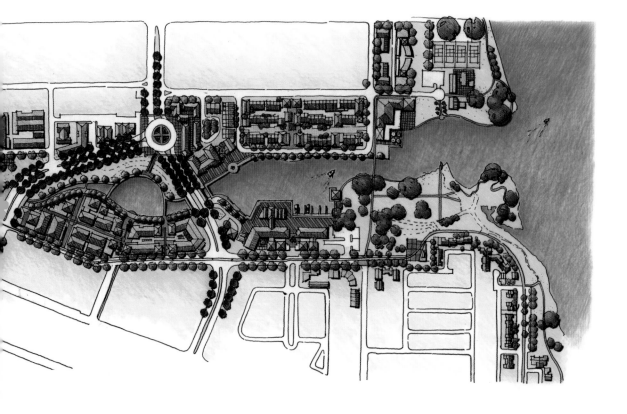

Claisebrook Main Drain, built to drain East Perth, dates from the early days of colonial settlement in the 1840s. The area has experienced a mixed destiny. The settlement's original rubbish tip was located here, and also the first acclimatisation garden in Perth, where exotic plants were harboured before being planted out. Aboriginal people called the area the Starlight Motel, retreating here following a nightly 6pm curfew that barred them from the city.

The area became a marginal location for small industry, concrete batching, a gas works, a sewerage treatment plant and was highly polluted.

The Better Cities programme (1988–1991) provided federal government funding for regenerating inner-city infrastructure and cleaning up pollution. Claisebrook was ripe for transformation. Polluted groundwater seepage and radioactive fly ash were removed and the watercourse sealed. The vaulted drain, which continues to carry stormwater, was fed into a series of shallow ponds lined with limestone, with hard landscape treatment up to the edges, enabling people to enjoy direct contact with the water. The water, constantly moving from pond to pond, is used for irrigation.

In designing a new park around the armature of the drain on a brownfield site, an objective was to establish links to the city centre and the Swan River. Protected by the surrounding buildings from winds that buffet the city, the park is a sheltered enclave that invites strolling and evokes the chequered urban history of its past and is a focal point for the new development.

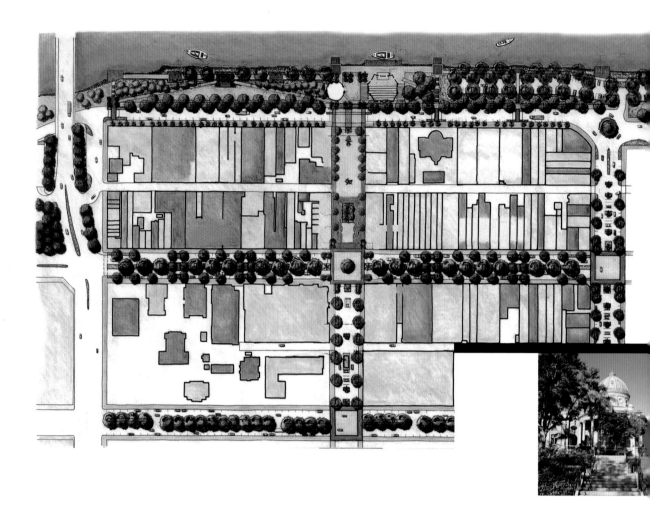

Rockhampton town centre and river park, Queensland

4.8

In 1997 Tract won an Australian design
competition to design Rockhampton's
central streetscape. This well-established
nineteenth-century country town
north of Brisbane has many fine Arts and
Crafts/neoclassical civic buildings.
But the centre had declined: shopping
activity was killed off in the 1980s
when the main street was closed to create
a pedestrian mall, robbing the town
centre of traffic. Tract reinstituted
the traditional shopping street typology
to reinvigorate the central commercial
heart. Subsequently, the adjacent
neglected River Park along the Fitzroy
River was upgraded with a boardwalk,
successfully refocusing the town
on its riverfront and creating a popular
promenade that incubates an outdoor
café culture and provides a central place
for socialising and family recreation.

Dandenong Mall, Dandenong, Victoria

4·9

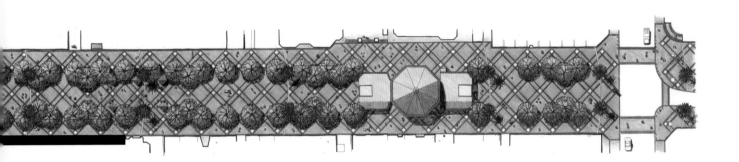

Landscape has the capacity to endow a sense of local identity through image-making overlaid with local ecology and culture. In 1988 Dandenong, a major regional centre, held a design competition for a city mall to regenerate the central retail core. The winning design by Tract draws on Dandenong's history as a rural market town. Circulation of the old run-down central district is revived with new vistas and pedestrian connections. The regular grid of the city is continued into the new open-air mall created by the partial closure of the main street, and the grid/memory is reflected in the dynamic paving patterning. Large palms immediately establish a new urban character, while as smaller trees mature, a growing sense of place will develop gradually.

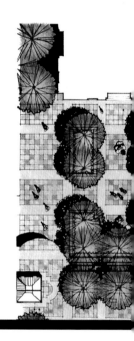

Forrest Place, Perth, Western Australia

4.10

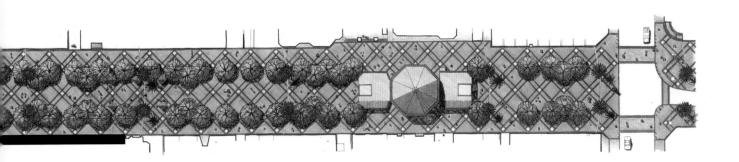

Landscape has the capacity to endow
a sense of local identity through image-
making overlaid with local ecology
and culture. In 1988 Dandenong,
a major regional centre, held a design
competition for a city mall to regenerate
the central retail core. The winning
design by Tract draws on Dandenong's
history as a rural market town.
Circulation of the old run-down central
district is revived with new vistas and
pedestrian connections. The regular
grid of the city is continued into the
new open-air mall created by the partial
closure of the main street, and the
grid/memory is reflected in the dynamic
paving patterning. Large palms
immediately establish a new urban
character, while as smaller trees
mature, a growing sense of place will
develop gradually.

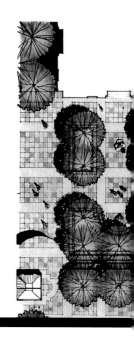

Forrest Place, Perth, Western Australia

4.10

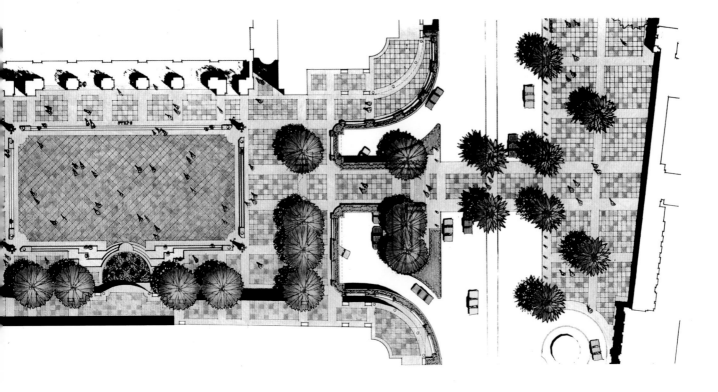

Perth is built on a sand dune, the city laid out in long narrow blocks between a railway line on one side and the Swan River on the other. Forrest Place acts as a gateway to the city centre, and it has been the main ceremonial precinct for more than 100 years. The objectives of the redevelopment were to attract people from the railway station into the city centre by drawing them through Forrest Place, and to create an active public space where both small gatherings and large rallies can be equally accommodated.

The plaza, more than 1 hectare, is built over a basement car park. It is surrounded by sandstone colonial buildings, including the General Post Office (no longer in operation).

The redeveloped public space forms a series of outdoor rooms of different sizes, the paving patterning responding to pedestrian desire lines and the surrounding built context. The Place feels enclosed and intimate and offers a variety of spatial experiences and gathering places.

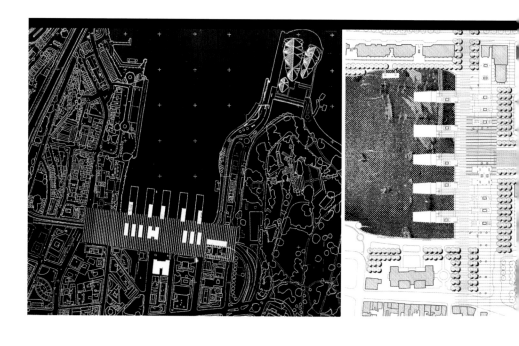

Circular Quay, Sydney, New South Wales

4.11

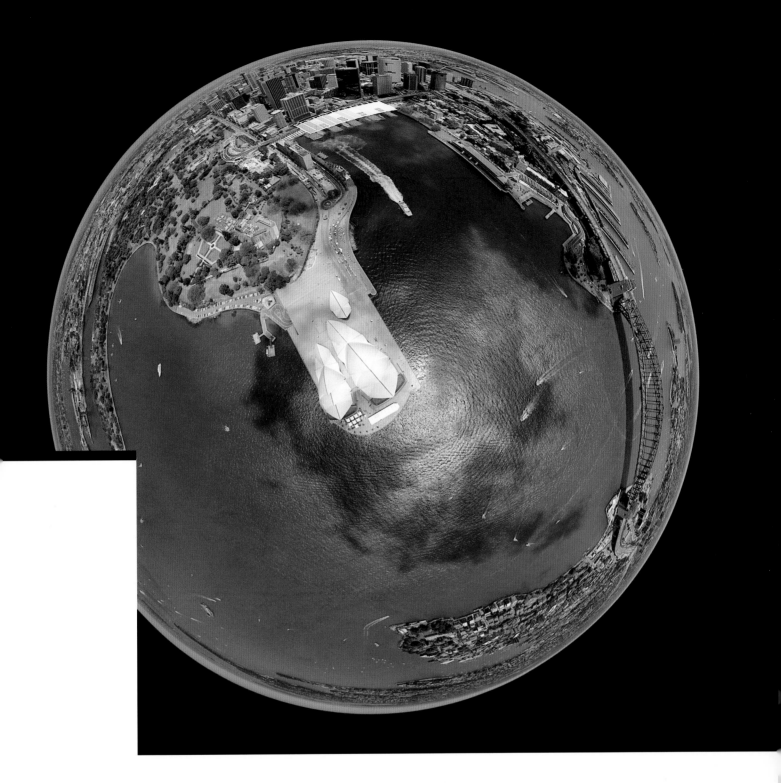

Tract Consultants, in collaboration with the architects, won equal first place in a national design competition in 1995 for Sydney's Circular Quay. The scheme establishes a concourse of retail spaces and public terraces that acts as a grandstand for viewing the theatre of the Harbour. The concourse runs from the Harbour Bridge to the Opera House, defining the pedestrian circuit between them.

The design reinforces the Quay's vital role as Sydney's major transport interchange. It retains the (contentious) raised freeway and railway that physically deprive the city of direct connection to the waterfront. The built elements at ground level are reorganised to increase visual and physical connections with the city.

the new private park

large scale_____
is not just associated_____
time-related_____

in landscape design
with size. It is also

The term 'landscape architecture' suggests the scale of the landscape itself. And landscape architects have always been concerned with expressing this larger scale. The eighteenth-century gardens (or more accurately, land compositions) of André Le Nôtre appropriated the whole landscape they are set in, and by implication too the unseen terrain beyond. Similarly, William Kent and Capability Brown measured the reach of their classical and romantic land compositions in terms of all that the eye could see, and more. Parks such as these were exclusive territories, designed to express personal wealth and power, as well as mythological and cosmological ideals: the entire landscape itself was none too large a canvas. But these days it is not aristocrats or the state or even the municipality that are responsible for establishing large scenic parks. It is more usually private enterprise that creates parks, not for the exclusive use of a privileged few but as commercial operations marketed to attract the general public. And the parks – holiday resorts, memorial gardens, wildlife sanctuaries, golf course estates – express not personal or civic grandeur but differently nuanced responses to a collective human desire to experience and be immersed in nature.

Large scale in landscape design is not just associated with size. It is also time-related. The typical time-scale for a park to reach full maturity is 50–100 years. It is impossible to sustain this evolution without continuous commitment to the intentions of the original design. In this, maintenance is critical: plants grow at different rates, and all the while the constant changes in vegetation must be managed and directed towards achieving the overall design vision. Complicated landscape designs relying on complex allusions and overlays of meaning are more likely to lose their identity and gradually fall apart, like chalk paintings on a pavement, than will a landscape design based on an armature of strong, simple ideas, readily understood, and able to endure through decades.

There are millions of reasons why people seek out the psychological and recreational benefits nature offers. Semi-rural golfing/residential estates package an experience of country life, wineries attract tourists seeking romantic rustic settings, memorial gardens offer spiritual solace through nature, holiday resorts provide balm to guests in the form of beautiful natural settings, and clean industrial parks include landscaped public recreational facilities. These are all new park types designed to furnish general and particular experiences of nature and in some way soothe the stresses of life while at the same time ministering to the commercial imperative for generating profits. Built by private enterprise, such parks serve both commercial and community ends.

5.0

Domaine Chandon, Yarra Valley, Victoria

5.1

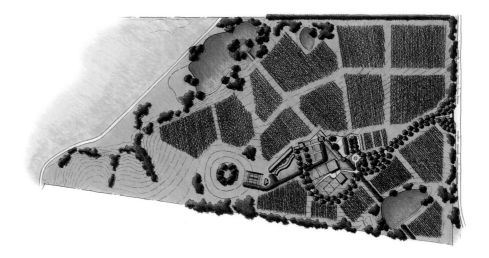

Vineyards once had no more significance in the rural landscape than the serried rows of orchards. To passing city-dwellers, they were as out of bounds as any other agribusiness. But that was before wine became big business, and before wineries were developed to market the wines. Dressed up as handsome vernacular farm buildings, wineries now are picturesquely sited overlooking hillsides radiating with vines. The passing public is invited in – lured by tours and tastings, three-star restaurants and shaded picnic tables – to sample and to buy wines authenticated by the romantic rustic setting where they were produced.

The Yarra Valley, not far from Melbourne, is an area famed for its wines. The Domaine Chandon vineyard is built around an existing Victorian farmhouse – remaining from the days when the estate was a dairy farm – with a new winemaking facility and restaurant designed by Allen Jack + Cottier.

Tract designed the landscape masterplan for the 160-hectare estate. It is an excellent example of what site planning can achieve. The landscape design is based on experiencing the estate. Domaine Chandon is also a tourist venue, and a narrative route describes to visitors the processes of wine making while allowing them to enjoy the countryside. In association with the viticulturist, Tract sited the blocks of grapes in optimal locations for growing conditions and views to an onsite lake and distant dramatic mountains.

Subtle topographical features are heightened. A large car park has been sunk below the ridge, preserving the landform. An existing pine and cypress shelter belt is extended into the landscape, and three large oaks are featured within a central grass courtyard space, framing and focusing the distant views.

Bunurong Memorial Park, Victoria

5.2

Bunurong Memorial Park, Victoria

5.2

The modern cemetery has been transformed from a sea of marble memorials into a type of park: a contemplative garden on a grand scale. Bunurong Memorial Park is set on 119 hectares of previously low waterlogged land. It is redolent of an eighteenth-century English romantic park, with lakes, vistas, and chapels instead of temples and follies. Water is significant in this landscape, connoting tranquillity and inclining people towards contemplation.

The sinuous water bodies thread throughout the park, intersecting with major paths and surrounded by the various garden areas, and creating peaceful views throughout Bunurong. The water is recycled from a local treatment plant and fed into scenic lakes and used also for irrigation.

Visitors are from different social and ethnic backgrounds, many grieving or infirm. Legibility is important, especially as this extremely large site carries a potential to bewilder first-time visitors uncertain of where they are meant to go, and many events are taking place simultaneously: wakes, memorial services, cremations, burials, as well as queuing to arrange burials or memorials, and visiting grave sites and memorials.

Each memorial garden has its own character. These distinctive places within the park help people understand their location in relation to the whole. Axial pathways denoting primary circulation also contribute to legibility.

Tract's landscape masterplan for Bunurong's flat terrain locates the roads and pathways, lakes, plots and memorial gardens, as well as buildings, and identifies landscape treatments for staged developments over 100 years.

Moonah Links golf course and resort development, Mornington Peninsula, Victoria

5.3

The moonah landscape of Rye on the Mornington Peninsula, south of Melbourne, is characterised by natural, grass-covered sand dune formations that suggest 'cups' across the land. Extensive grazing of the area over the past 150 years has degraded the natural sand dune terrain, although there are stands of remnant indigenous moonah vegetation and wildlife habitats.

In the late 1980s Tract planned cluster-based subdivisions of dwellings in suitable locations across a large site in this landscape, protecting identified scenic and environmentally significant areas by incorporating them into a golf course or in common property areas.

This entailed compiling an inventory of moonah tree stands and significant areas of landscape, as well as drainage patterns, soil composition, and solar and wind conditions.

Despite approval of an initial development in the late 1980s, the economic viability of the scheme was limited by the impost of maintaining a large land area in common ownership. Subsequently, however, an aging society seeking recreation-based living has presented the opportunity to integrate a larger recreational component into the development. Additional land was incorporated into the original site, enabling a model championship golf course with two courses, clubhouse, hotel and a 250-lot resort development, while maintaining the principles of the original site analysis and design response studies.

The additional land ensured enough open landscape to retain the integrity of the site and protect remnant stands of moonah vegetation.

A site-specific comprehensive development zone was developed and approved for this strategic project. All land use servicing issues were addressed and improved, with the development including road access, provision of sewer and water to the area and the closure of an adjoining poultry farm for incorporation into the site, thereby improving amenity to adjoining residents.

Moonah Links is now the home of Golf Australia, the 2003 Australian Open being the inaugural championship played on the site.

Moonah Links golf course and resort development, Mornington Peninsula, Victoria

5.4

Laguna Quays Whitsunday resort, Queensland

The landscape design of this 1850-hectare tropical resort is a watershed in the way that it departs from the prevalent commercial holiday vision of a lush Hawaiian paradise, exploiting instead an authentic local Australian tropical idiom. This was at first a matter of necessity. The large area and comparatively small budget precluded an exotic landscape: lush planting would have required importing tons of topsoil. However, by working with and celebrating the terrain – dry sclerophyll forest, thin soil, and rocky outcrops – it was possible to achieve the ambitious landscape brief within the budget.

Laguna Quays is on the tropical coast in a region of steep hills falling to the coastal plain. The waterfront was partly mangroves. It has been honeycombed to create a harbour, marina, and saltwater lagoon for swimming and snorkelling. The town centre, residences and golf course are dispersed in behind the coastal frontage.

The landscape design responds to the site, using indigenous grasses and trees to celebrate the gully topography, as well as rock from the site for stone walls. The masterplan established the water bodies and developed a network of catchment areas for water run-off, which is contained and recycled. Bright grassy fairways threading through the dark green native landscape create a distinct contrast to the bushland.

In highlighting and framing the bush in this way, the local vegetation appears special. Local plants are used also in picturesque ways, such as the bold massings of coastal pandanas palms that announce entries, creek-lines and gateways. The environmental landscape equally serves economic, ecological and aesthetic needs, and adds substantially to the value of the development.

Laguna Quays Whitsunday resort, Queensland

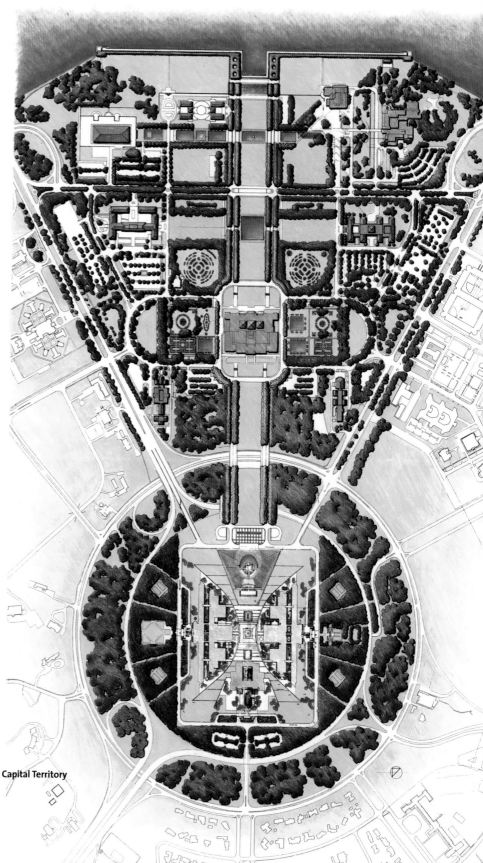

Parliamentary Triangle, Canberra, Australian Capital Territory

5.5 Australia's national capital, Canberra, was planned in the early nineteenth century by Walter Burley Griffin, a former associate of Frank Lloyd Wright, along the lines of an ideal garden city. Despite being an architect, Burley Griffin was denied the opportunity to consolidate any of his urban vision in built form. But his great and lasting contribution to the realisation of Canberra was to put into place the bones of the future city – the core land and water axes, the siting of major buildings, the landscape features, the roads – that would be fleshed out as the city came into being.

Despite construction of the city during the decades following World War II, Canberra still has key sites waiting to be finally developed. The Parliamentary Triangle is one such precinct. In December 1982 Tract and architects Denton Corker Marshall were appointed to develop landscape and site planning proposals for the Parliamentary Triangle, which includes the land axis taking in the new Parliament House, the Old Parliament House and the National Library, High Court and National Gallery.

Northcorp Industrial Park, Broadmeadows, Victoria

5.6

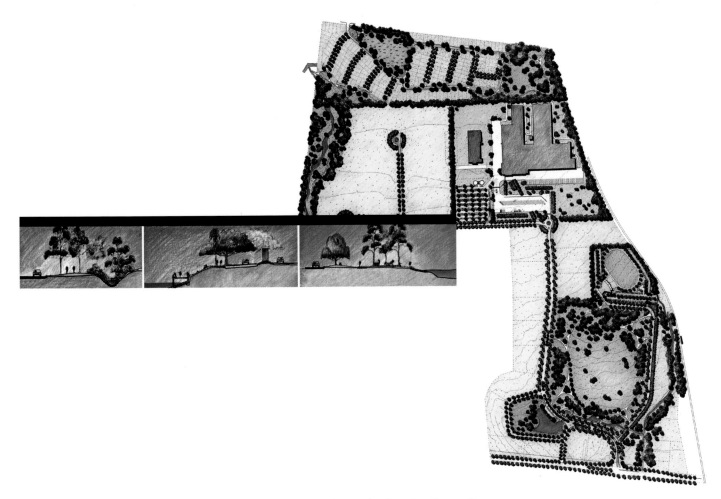

The idea of an industrial park within a recreational park setting, providing public open space, is perhaps paradoxical. However, Northcorp is a decentralised location for clean industry, head offices, a recreational/sporting complex (Melbourne Greyhound Racing headquarters and track) and a commercial distribution centre. The masterplanning also caters for the community with lakeside parks, and proposed childcare, restaurants and library.

The native landscape has been re-created on this formerly degraded site, originally an army camp on the outer edges of the city. The new park is planned and designed according to environmentally sustainable design principles. A wetland/creek adjoins one boundary, and the lower lying area once occupied by an old army sewerage treatment plant was reconfigured as the basis for the stormwater purification system. Stormwater run-off is channelled to the lake formed by settlement ponds, where it overflows and passes through a series of cascades which aerate and purify it before it is returned clean into the creek. The lake and cascades protect downstream areas from flooding and run-off pollution from the roadways, while at the same time creating a focal public recreational attraction. The wetlands and waterways are replanted with native species to attract native birds and regenerate the natural ecology.

The site planning set up the overall road structure, which is flexible to allow the subdivision of large or small lots, depending on market demand and open space. Remnant stands of grey box and native grasses are retained, and scenic drives and pathways wind through the landscape. A childcare centre and library will be built on the site as part of the communal facilities.

The entry road is set down low, with berms on either side and lined with trees, to dramatise the experience of entry. Throughout this park, the utilitarian is given a scenic vision. And somewhere in the midst of it, industry quietly flourishes.

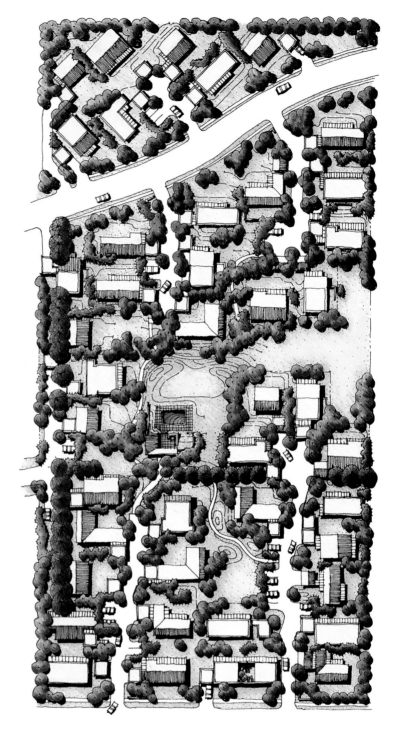

Vermont Park, Melbourne, Victoria

5·7

Tract was responsible for site planning
and landscape design for a cluster
subdivision with 43 houses on a 4-hectare
site, including community facilities such
as a swimming pool. The intention was
to provide an alternative to typical
subdivision development, at comparable
densities, with detached houses.

the campus operates as a civic and intensifying experience of the and the activities of meeting, socialising at the heart

social condenser,

public realm

and discourse
of university life

The Cloister and the Agora

6.0

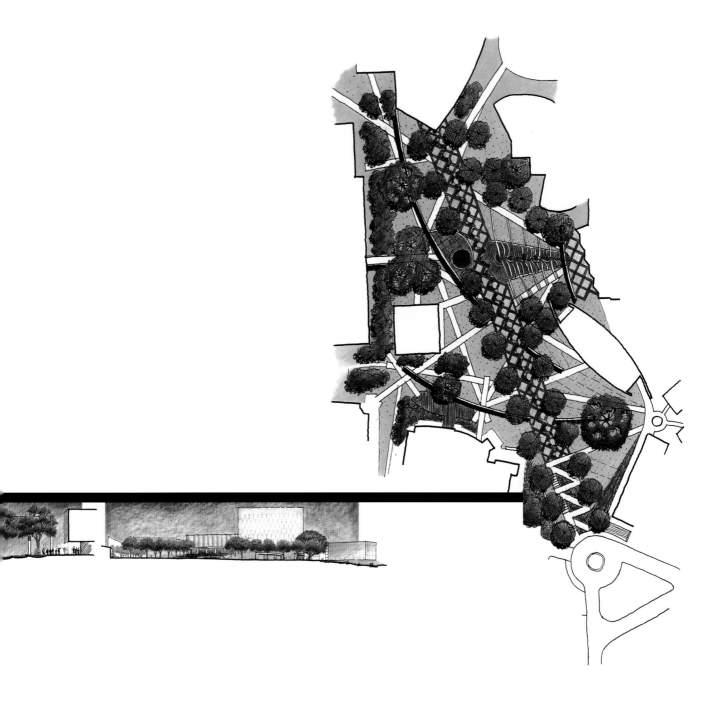

The existing campus at Burwood, an outer suburb of Melbourne, was both dismal and confusing. Large buildings from different eras had been sited without reference to each other or to objectives of urban legibility and place-making. An iconic new building designed by Wood Marsh signals a strong positive identity for the university from the highway. Yet on the ground, unrelated buildings could not in themselves generate order and clarity throughout the campus, or form a central gathering place. The goals of Tract's landscape strategy were to unify and give meaning to the disparate built form elements and open spaces, and to establish one main focal point for the campus.

A design solution often lies in subtracting existing elements. Small-scale nondescript demountable buildings were cleared away in order to open up a wide swathe and create a strong axis running from the entry gate through to the library, the intellectual core of the institution. The axis establishes an ordering armature to the campus and makes sense of the faculty buildings located along it.

Towards the campus centre, the axis becomes a wide public promenade criss-crossed by many paths. A stylised amphitheatre in front of the student union and a fountain spilling down the slope signal this as the university's centre. Here the site has an 8-metre cross fall. Initially Tract identified the natural catchment and drainage of stormwater into a creek as a possible

design generator. This ecological idea was translated into the principal design feature, the flow-form fountain – recalling the fish rill of the Villa Lante at Bagnaia, designed by Vignola in 1566 – where water swirls down a runnel into bilobal forms that oxygenate and purify it. The fountain simultaneously announces the new symbolic heart of the campus, negotiates the changes in level down the hill, and collects and cleans run-off catchment water, raising the utilitarian process to an aesthetic expression.

The utilitarian is also raised to an aesthetic level by the geometric pattern of crossing paths that demarcate desire lines. The diagonal

paths recall Thomas Jefferson's tactic in laying out the University of Virginia in 1817; he waited a year before locating the paths across the central green, until winter when he could observe where people typically walked by seeing their tracks in the snow. The graphic use of vector paths is characteristic of Tract's work. The paths not only provide routes and short cuts, but also define particular places for meeting and sitting, and by breaking down scale, they humanise the larger public space. Different decorative treatments of the hard paving also help to define distinct places. The coloured broken tiles of a section of paving make reference to Gaudi and contribute an organic element to the spiky geometry.

Queensland University of Technology, Gardens Point Campus, Brisbane, Queensland

6.2

The densely built campus was initially planned as a technical college, with no grand pretensions. Despite its spectacular peninsular site defined by a bend in the Brisbane River and by the luxuriant Botanic Gardens, and located just blocks from the city centre, the campus developed as a dowdy utilitarian agglomeration of early- to mid-twentieth-century institutional dark brick buildings, with a high wire fence isolating it from the adjacent gardens. Over the decades, the spaces of the constrained site were filled in ad hoc according to necessity,

without benefit of social or aesthetic standards. In the subtropical climate, the prevalence of hard paving surfaces often made the experience of being outdoors uncomfortable.

The central ordering idea of Tract's 1995 masterplan is legibility. The density of buildings makes it impossible to see where one is headed, so there had to be alternative ways to understand the campus; one way was through the circulation paths, another was signalling the nodes, using tall foxtail palms. The objective was to transform the shambles of buildings, light courts, service yards and alleyways into a coherent site that projects the vision of a dynamic university.

The design strategy is opportunistic: any slight widening of the space between buildings is transformed into a place. Sunshine and shade – both vital for comfortable outdoor living throughout the year – are deployed to create outdoor 'lounges' where people meet, relax, and even study. These places – rather than the nondescript buildings – form active nodes that thread along the circulation routes and stitch the campus together. The campus becomes a labyrinth of social encounters within intimate garden spaces.

Main Drive_Queensland University of Technology, Gardens Point Campus, Brisbane, Queensland

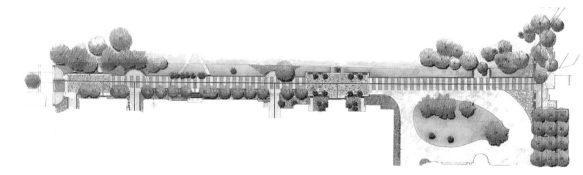

The Yard_Queensland University of Technology, Gardens Point Campus, Brisbane, Queensland

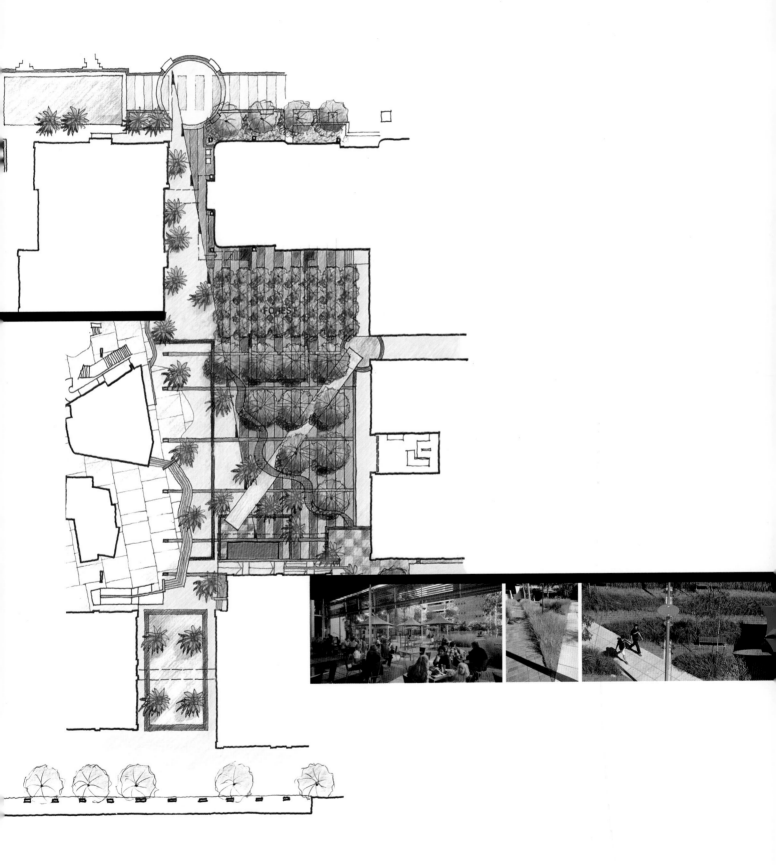

FOREST

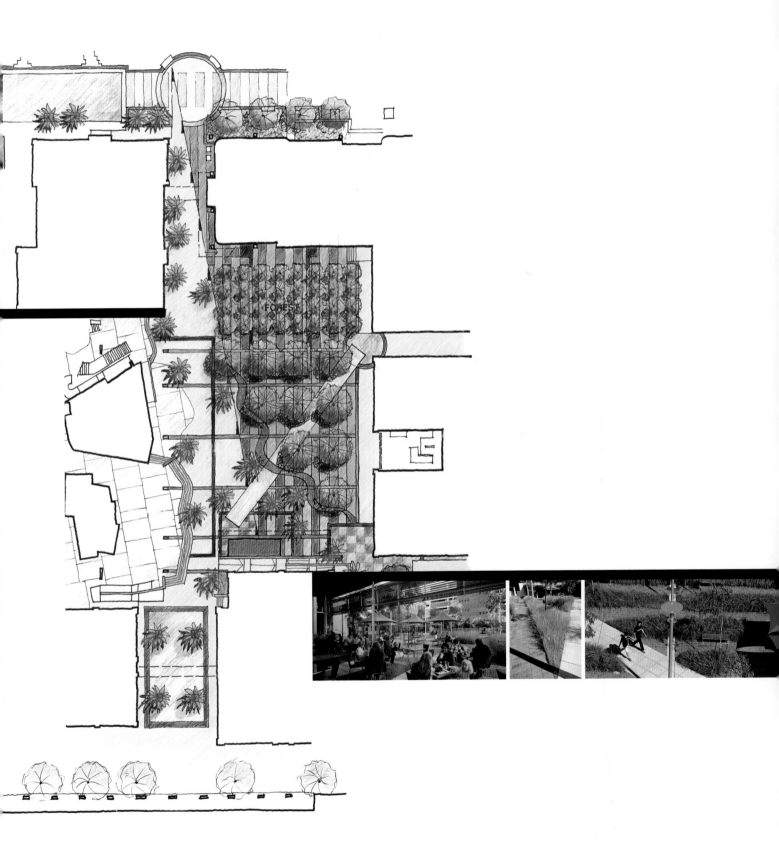

FOREST

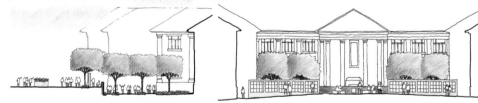

Library Podium_Queensland University of Technology, Gardens Point Campus, Brisbane, Queensland

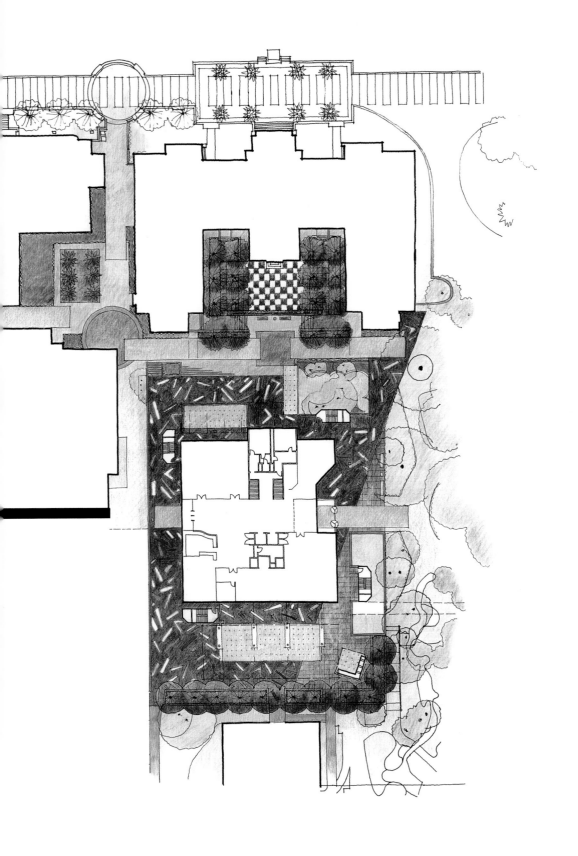

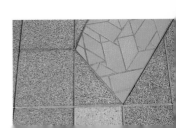

Union Court_Queensland University of Technology, Gardens Point Campus, Brisbane, Queensland

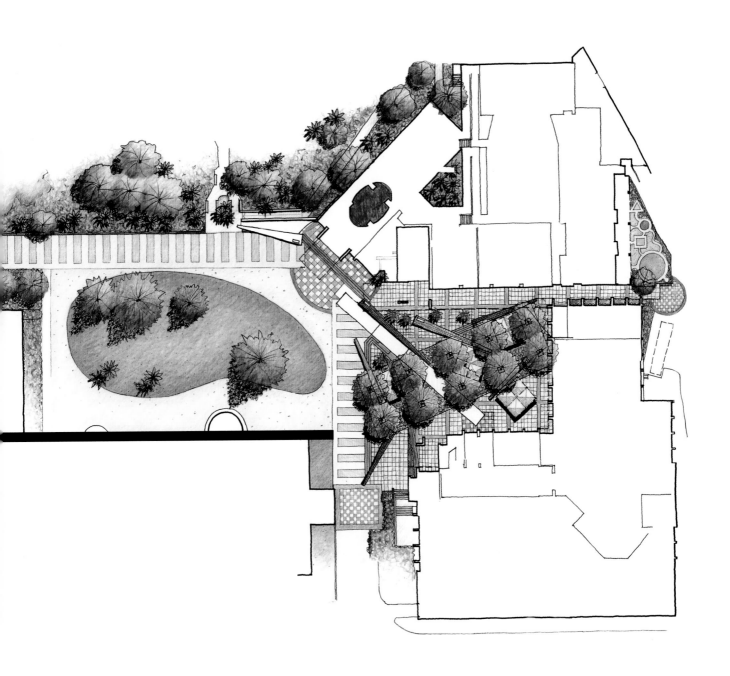

Bridge Link_Queensland University of Technology, Gardens Point Campus, Brisbane, Queensland

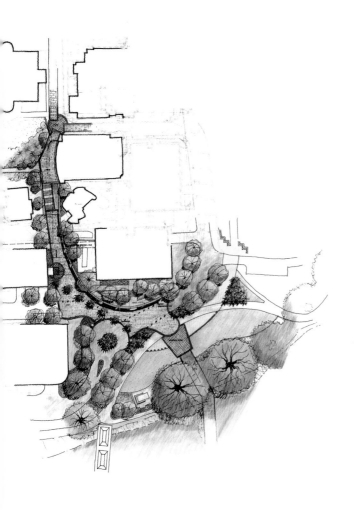

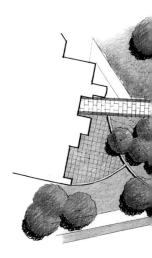

Queensland University of Technology, Kelvin Grove Campus, Brisbane, Queensland

6.3

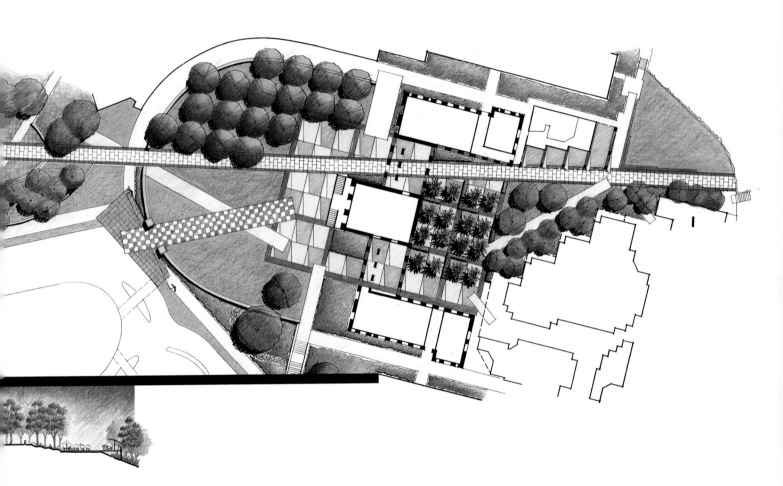

The context was unpromising, the budget very small. In rescuing the suburban campus, the principal issues were legibility and place-making. The site is perched on top of a steep ridge, the buildings crammed together on the available land, like a hill town. A car park cluttered the main place of arrival, and the buildings lacked presence. In order to dress up the front door appropriately and establish a public space – an agora – on the cramped site, the first task was to recover the parking area, by removing the cars, and to create the setting for gathering and a new arrival sequence. From here the pedestrian spine linking the campus sets up a diagonal axis connecting the student union, library and cafés. The axis cuts right through the main building; this was achieved by excising part of the ground floor to connect with a small existing courtyard behind and then collect the other campus elements.

The courtyard was previously a dank space overshadowed by native trees; they were replaced by an ordered grove of tall palms, allowing in sunshine and creating a formal court in keeping with the formality of the surrounding heritage buildings.

The tactics are essentially those of garden making. At the small scale of the garden, the landscape architect has only form and pattern to work with, and here Tract employs a painterly approach. The effect is to establish, with minimal intervention and at minimal cost, a new presence and identity for the campus.

Queensland University of Technology, Kelvin Grove Campus, Brisbane, Queensland

Monash University, Clayton Campus, Victoria

6.4

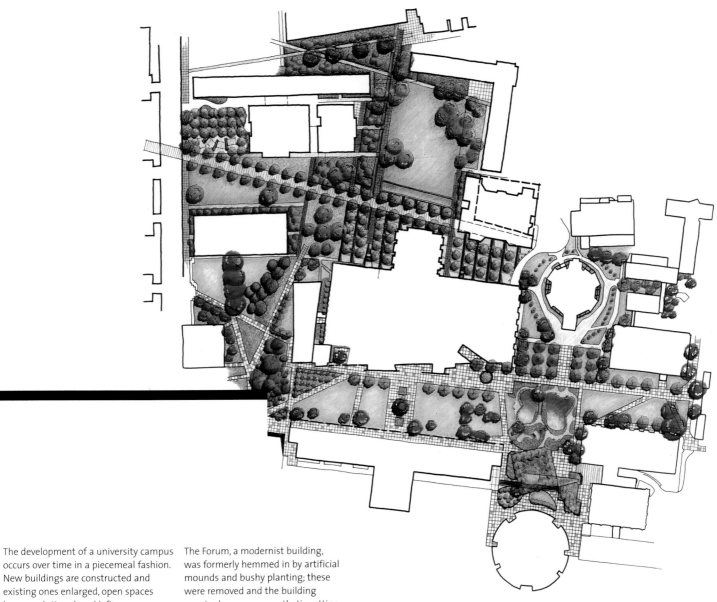

The development of a university campus occurs over time in a piecemeal fashion. New buildings are constructed and existing ones enlarged, open spaces become cluttered, and leftover passages are re-made into utilitarian courtyards or thoroughfares. Here the task has been to simplify and dignify an uninspiring interstitial space between several buildings and create a ceremonial pathway placed on axis with a significant stained-glass window by Leonard French in Blackwood Hall.

The Forum, a modernist building, was formerly hemmed in by artificial mounds and bushy planting; these were removed and the building acquired a more sympathetic setting in keeping with its architectural character. The landscape design pares away extraneous elements to clarify and unify the open space, establish legibility, and connect the different buildings facing onto it.

building settings

or genius loci,
a potent, if fragile, force

7.0

Bendigo Art Gallery, Bendigo, Victoria

7.2

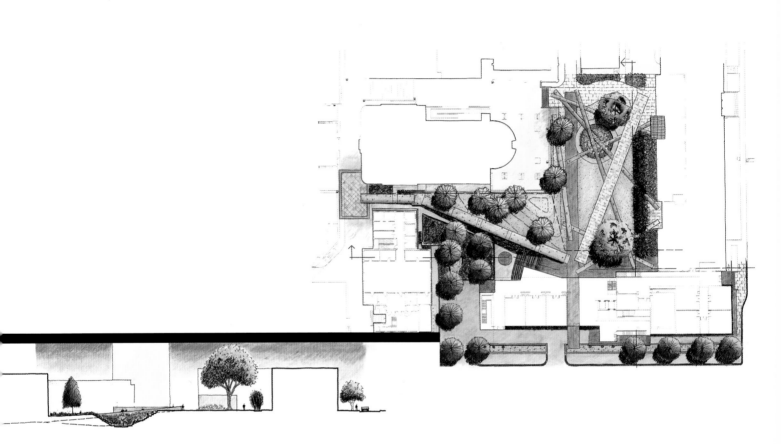

The University of Melbourne is located in a prime, leafy, cosmopolitan area within walking distance of the centre of the city. Along one of its principal boundaries, Swanston Street, the University has raised its profile by placing public cultural institutions and entries into the campus.

The Sidney Myer Asia Centre is a new academic, cultural and business centre. A scrappy car park was cleared to make way for the building designed by Nation Fender Katsalidis. It reinforces the University's presence on the street and creates a gateway. A major sculptural wall in rusted Cor-ten by the late Akio Makigawa signals the Centre and also entry to the campus.

Tract's landscape design transforms the original car park from an expanse of bitumen into a stylised garden setting that evokes the calm order and serenity of Asian gardens. The focal point of the space is the linear water feature framing an elevated lemon-scented lawn and defining a bluestone pathway leading into the courtyard from Swanston Street. A gently rippling reflection pond flows through a bluestone trough into a lower pond. A line of black bamboo frames the courtyard lawn and creates a green veil to the lecture theatres overlooking it.

Asia Centre, University of Melbourne, Victoria

7.1

When Gertrude Stein berated her boring Midwest home town for having 'no there there', she was talking about sense of place – or rather, from her cosmopolitan perspective, the absence of a sense of place. Sense of place, or genius loci, is generally a potent, if fragile, force. It consists of the sum of many parts: landform and terrain, buildings, trees and flowers, animals, birds, insects, colours, climate, winds, sounds, smells – the multifarious characteristics that together make a place particular and give it a distinct flavour. Genius loci is not immutable: it can easily be bulldozed out of existence in a single move, or be more gradually eroded by the persistent depredations of development. The value of subtle local traits is easily overlooked, until they are lost.

Landscape design has always played a major role in creating scenographic backdrops and settings for buildings and places. The task of designers of the environment is to reconstruct – or construct – a sense of place where development has either altered or obliterated what existed previously. How this task is approached depends on many issues concerning place: physical issues such as ecology, context, planning, urban legibility; cultural and social issues such as identity, authenticity, conservation, community; economic issues such as jobs, commercial prestige, tourism. Landscape design has a social impact as much as aesthetic and environmental effects. Its purpose is to knit together a place, to make connections, signal major nodes and entries, establish legible circulation patterns, enhance identity. In establishing a physical vision for a place, the designer sifts through these often competing values and makes decisions about which ones will best contribute to the development of an appropriate setting.

Landscape Architecture

7.0

or genius loci,
a potent, if fragile, force

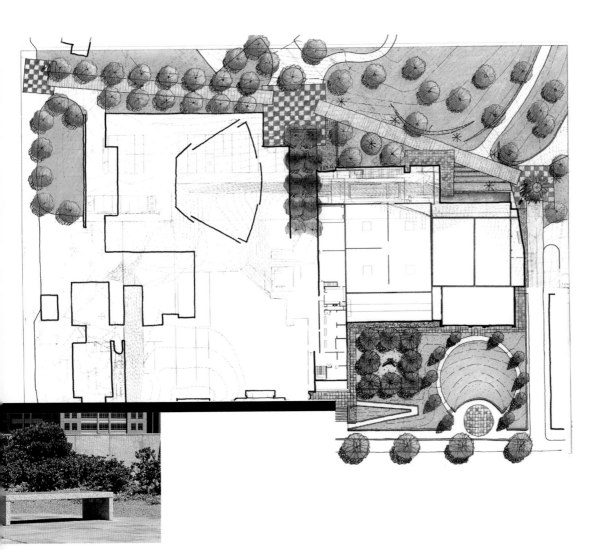

Bendigo is a major provincial town. Tract collaborated with architects Nation Fender Katsalidis in the redevelopment of a historic brick building into an art gallery precinct. The landscape creates an entry experience and a series of formal settings for the complex that includes a sculpture court, amphitheatre and garden. Each setting is framed by a symmetrical, axial composition, in keeping with the civic character of the old and new built elements.

174_   Capalaba town centre, Queensland

7.3

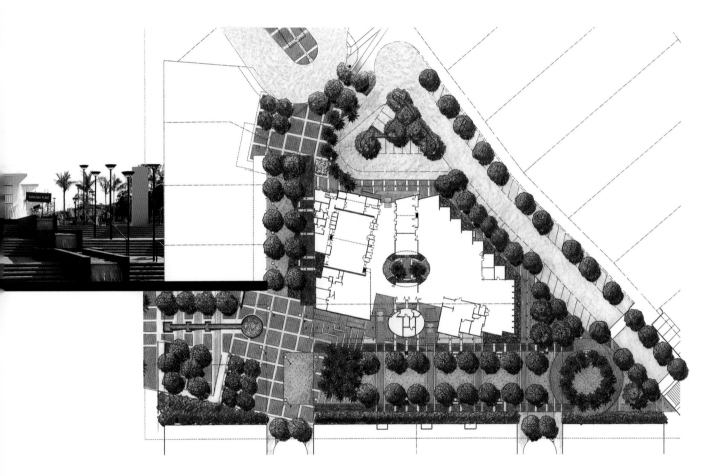

Many small towns in south-eastern Queensland have found themselves suddenly swallowed up by a rising tide of suburban development as a result of sustained population influx. Capalaba was formerly an outlying highway junction. When Brisbane's suburban sprawl reached the sparse village, the local council decided to arrest strip development and establish a town centre to concentrate commercial and community activities. There was no community infrastructure, so a new community building with council offices and a library were located between two existing shopping centres to encourage traffic between them and anchor the new node. A town centre in miniature was established from nothing.

Capalaba's straggling streetscape projected a nondescript identity. Tract prepared an urban masterplan and streetscape design guidelines for the town centre and approach roads. Lush planting and bold paving contribute formality and order. In the sub-tropical climate, the provision of an 'art' park and street trees contribute a microclimate of cooler shaded pathways, ameliorating the effects of the harsh sun while encouraging gatherings of the local community.

Australian Geological Survey Organisation, Canberra, Australian Capital Territory

7·4

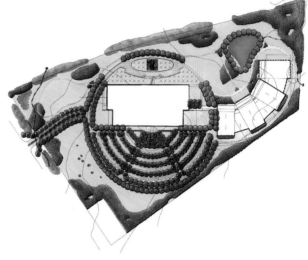

The AGSO complex lies like a scorpion across the 18-hectare greenfield site, the curving 'tail' a series of three-storey blocks with courtyards within. Canberra experiences a climate of extremes: very hot in summer and prone to frosts during winter. Tract designed a mannered landscape setting for the institution, using geometry to order the grounds and locate car parking and express entries and key nodes. The planting regime also has a climatic impact: deciduous exotics allow winter sun into the buildings and shade interiors from summer sun; and windbreaks of native species help protect the site.

The stormwater management infrastructure of retention basins becomes the basis of wetland habitats, with aquatic species selected to soften the visual impact of stormwater structures.

In keeping with the geological role of the AGSO, various internal gardens express abstracted terrains and landscapes encountered by the scientists. An arid terrain in the library courtyard is symbolic of dry desert creeks; it is balanced by a courtyard with a wet tropical theme. Earth mounds and rocks are placed in bold compositions around the site to reinforce original rock outcrops and to dramatise the landscape.

National Tennis Centre, Melbourne, Victoria

7.8

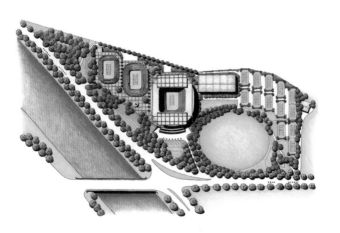

This extensive office and mixed-use
development on the south bank
of the Yarra includes nine buildings,
open space areas, a large quay
linked to the river, pedestrian bridge,
and substantial peripheral landscape
development. The design of hard
and soft surface treatments, features
and furniture demanded resolution
of complex technical issues,
and was undertaken in collaboration
with architects Godfrey and Spowers
and the engineers.

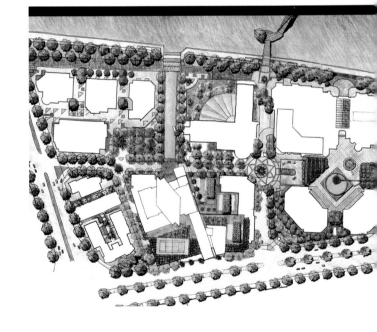

Riverside Quay, Melbourne, Victoria

7·7

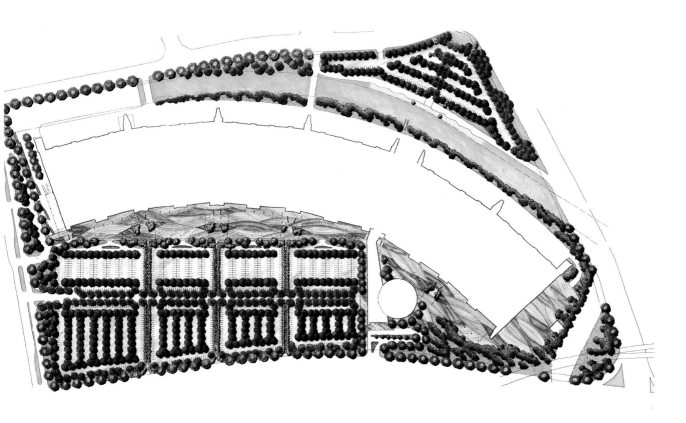

One of the world's largest exhibition complexes is located on a previously derelict 29-hectare site, transformed by over 33,000 ground covers, trees, shrubs and palms. In the tropical climate, the dense landscape provides a welcome green setting for the exhibition halls and a pleasant microclimate for the various integrated indoor/outdoor spaces. Efficient wayfinding is important, especially in a public complex of this scale – over 600 metres long – and the landscape treatment promotes legibility and helps to humanise the impact of the built form. Another task is to express an appropriately festive identity for the exhibition complex, and to create attractive places where people can rest or socialise.

Singapore Convention Centre, Singapore

7.6

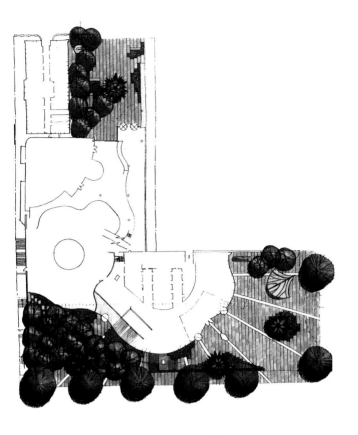

Shell House, Melbourne, Victoria

7.5

The headquarters building designed
by Harry Seidler occupies a prominent
corner site on the edge of the city.
The entry court is dominated by Seidler's
signature incorporation of a large-scale
modern art work complementing
his architecture. Equally, the landscape
is designed to complement the
architecture. Tract designed the gardens,
paving, planters and roof-top garden
beds. The landscape is experienced
on the ground as well as from above
as a pictorial element. Wind studies
of the site helped ensure that turbulence
in the open spaces is minimised through
judicious tree and shrub plantings.
The planting follows a modernist
expression that establishes an elegant
urban setting.

Tract prepared the site analysis and
landscape appraisal for the National
Tennis Centre in Flinders Park,
as well as the developed landscape
design and documentation for the entire
precinct, including the concourse level,
Old Scotch Oval and the Batman Avenue-
Swan Street frontages. Timing was
critical and works were fast-tracked.
An earth berm running the full length
of the Tennis Centre site reduces
the visual impact of its service area and
ensures the site is integrated into
its larger park context along the Yarra
River in Melbourne's Garden Precinct.

Melbourne Cricket Ground (MCG), Melbourne, Victoria

7.9

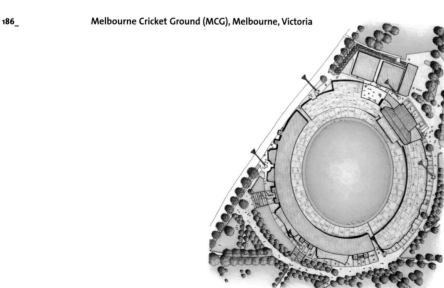

The MCG is hallowed territory in Melbourne. The cricket ground sits in the midst of extensive parkland. Tract's urban design and landscape treatment for the MCG surrounds includes the Great Southern Stand, Northern Stand and the Gallery of Sport, and integrates the stadium with one of Melbourne's oldest and most important parks. The landscape design includes bold tree planting, simple, elegant paving, and areas for crowd massing and service vehicles.

the road

The scream of
is dulled by the_____
which on their_____
from the road,_____

the highway

noise barrier walls

reverse side, away

are hidden behind trees

The highway that joins distant points on the map also cleaves an impenetrable barrier between the two sides of territory it severs. It creates two distinct kinds of landscape experience. The driver on the high-speed road sees the black traffic lanes ahead, the blurred vegetated berms and verges, and the steep walls of noise baffles cocooning the road corridor and at the same time concealing the fabric of suburbia beyond. The road occupies a landscape of detachment: abstracted from its original context, placeless yet powerfully present and immediate, experienced as a dynamic continuum, singular in its purpose, and conceptually endless. In contrast, the resident, pedestrian or cyclist on the other side of the noise baffles sees and smells and hears a natural environment. The scream of the highway is dulled by the noise barrier walls which on their reverse side, away from the road, are hidden behind trees.

This other landscape experience is complex, tactile, unfolding as a sequence of different settings and places, sequestered and sylvan.

The highway cuts a disjunctive section across the terrain: the road corridor – defined by the containing noise walls and berms – abruptly abuts on each side the natural topography of gullies, hills, creeks and houses. Two different kinds of landscape treatment are in play here: the abstracted, artificial, functionalist corridor containing the road, and the bucolic or reconstituted parkland environment of the territory on either side. But even this 'natural' topography is an artificial construct, with remediated parkland stitching together existing remnants of degraded bush left over from decades of inhabitation, pressure and pollution. Road and territory, then, are not so much opposites as two faces of human intervention on the landscape.

Two Sides of the Road

8.0

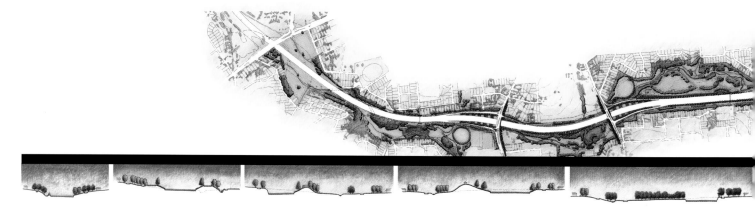

Eastern Freeway extension, Melbourne, Victoria

8.1

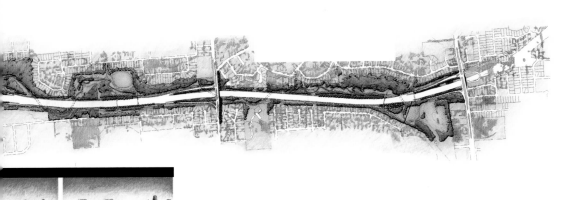

When Tract, as part of the VicRoads design team, gave the 7-kilometre Eastern Freeway extension an aesthetic landscape overlay, the design question it investigated was how to engender the experience of the road. Tract explored two ideas of a single dichotomy: the speed experienced by motorists, and the slow unfolding sensations of people strolling in a park.

Along the bitumen corridor of the freeway the traffic roars on, drivers intent on nudging across into the correct lane to peel off at their junctions. The landscape treatment enhances the mundane experience of freeway driving by being sufficiently varied and pleasant to help drivers stay alert. The drive becomes an episode of flickering rhythms of hard and soft landscape and blurs of muted colour and texture. Along the verges, against the concrete noise barrier walls, earth mounds undulate as a continuous flowing topography, reinforcing the perception of speed. In a painterly, modernist abstract planting composition recalling Burle-Marx, the verges are carpeted by extended stretches of single native plant species that change in composition from riverine to dryland species as one moves up the valley. This environment of the road expresses the high-speed experience of seamless momentum.

Although the proposal to construct a freeway extension caused community consternation, the road became the opportunity to transform an area of neglected bushland into a linear local park, a positive outcome for the community. The route cuts through a water catchment basin, and the creek here had become a degraded stormwater drain feeding directly into the Yarra River. A standard means of containing and directing polluted stormwater is to barrel it through 2-metre diameter concrete pipes. Tract proposed a simpler remedial strategy for stormwater management, channelling the creek into a series of naturalist ponds and forming a bush park alongside the road. The simpler strategy has many advantages: ecological, financial, aesthetic, social. Ecologically it made sense to reinforce the eroded gully and to channel run-off into settling ponds; plants growing in the water absorb pollutants and oil. Financially this was cheaper by millions of dollars than

piping the water: planting represents just 5–10 per cent of a construction budget. The remedial solution has aesthetic and social benefits too, creating a public park through the valley. Pathways link up with the extensive Yarra River track, enabling people to bicycle to work.

This area can never be returned to its pristine bush state. But a memory of its original condition has been reconstructed using indigenous species. Over 4 million native plants were installed, sourced from local seed. And over 4 kilometres of creek bed was re-established and lined with local rocks to create a 'natural' creek base. Small fish that had disappeared returned to the area when the water quality improved and the landscape regenerated.

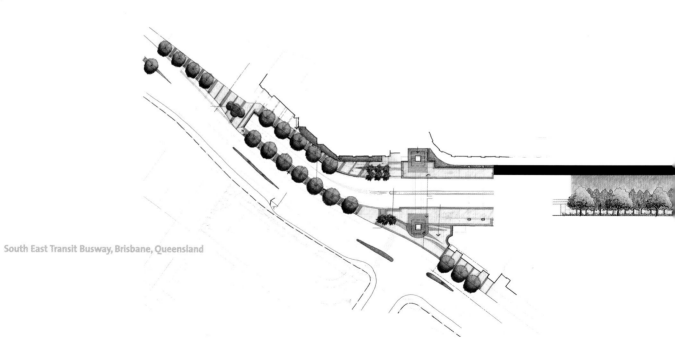

South East Transit Busway, Brisbane, Queensland

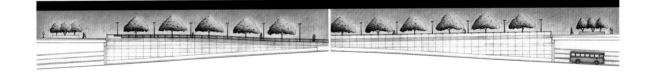

Urban freeways, Melbourne, Sydney, Brisbane

8.3

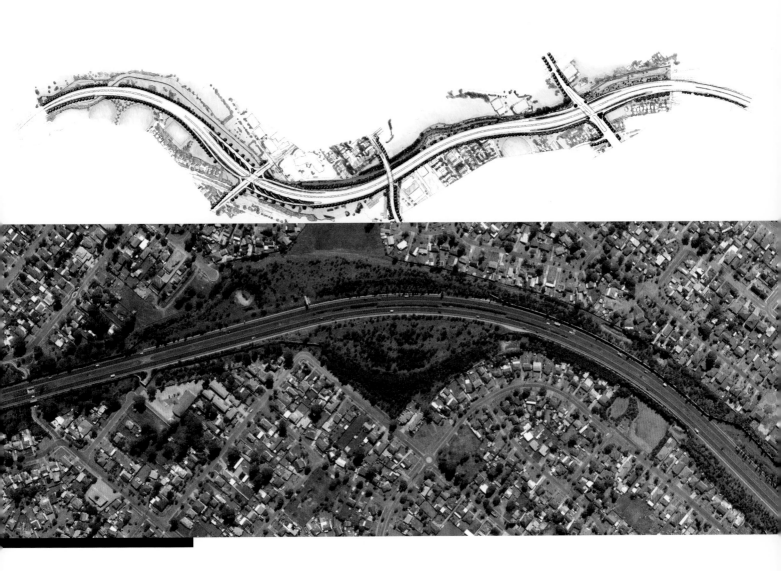

The Toorak Road to High Street segment of the South-Eastern Arterial (known as the Monash Freeway) in Melbourne's south-eastern suburbs was a jumble of at-grade road crossings and soulless landscape treatments. The design (1994–1996) creates a stylised structured landscape within the noise walls that evolved from the grain of the development along the road route; mounding and freeform planting softens the freeway from the suburban and parkland surrounds. The design and documentation of a large indigenous wetland area on Gardiners Creek was part of the works. Tract worked with the local community to ensure the intrusion of the freeway was minimised and the development of recreational parkland maximised.

Tract landscaped Sydney's first tollway (the M5, 15 kilometres, 1991–ongoing) which was completed in 1994. The M5 connects the Hume Highway at Liverpool with King George's Road at Beverly Hills, the route passing through many diverse natural landscapes and suburban contexts. Tract concentrated on the amelioration of the environmental impact of the project, devising techniques to economically establish and sustain natural vegetation systems along the entire corridor. Subsequently Tract was engaged in the planning and design of a 6-kilometre extension of the motorway, completed in 1996, and continues involvement with monitoring and auditing the landscape management.

The Gateway motorway extension (1995–1997) is 10.5 kilometres of new road joining the South-Eastern Freeway to the Logan Motorway, south of Brisbane, with a toll plaza at the junction. Local authority disagreements concerning the route resulted in the road having a big kink. Cuttings were necessary through the rocky hills, up to 20 metres deep, and the batters required stabilisation and revegetation. Rehabilitation of sensitive areas has been carried out using native grasses and trees, sourcing seed from the nearby intact open eucalypt forest. In addition, Tract designed the creek diversions, equestrian underpasses, fauna paths, and infrastructure for water management. The overall objective was to minimise the environmental impact of the road on the landscape.

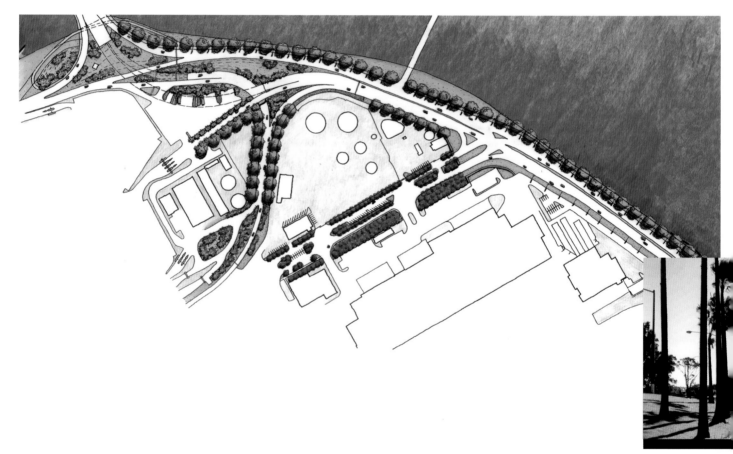

Infrastructure landscape_Sydney International Airport, Sydney, New South Wales

8.4

Through the late 1990s Tract designed the landscape components of a number of the infrastructure projects at the airport, as well as for the private interests adjoining the airport.

In the lead-up to the 2000 Olympics, Tract designed the new streetscapes for the Domestic Terminal and the gateway to the International Terminal.

Geelong Road, Princes Freeway, Victoria

8.5

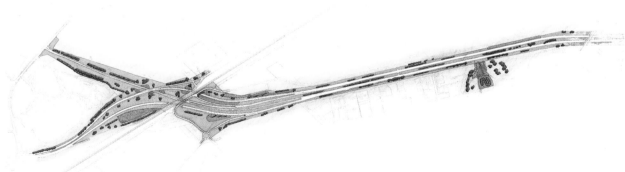

As the major arterial linking Geelong with Melbourne, the Princes Freeway is more than just a road: it acts as the gateway to Werribee, Geelong and the Western District, famous for its wool. But the long, straight road is flat, drab and monotonous. Overgrown shrubs alongside verges block wider distant landscape views. The drive does not inspire appreciation of the land or signal sense of arrival.

The gently undulating landforms are sparsely treed. This is mostly open, grazing, pastoral country.

The design response is to engage and enhance the rural spirit of the expansive landscape by breaking the visual monotony of the road journey. The overgrown shrubs are removed, releasing the expansive views out to the wider country, and to features in the landscape such

as the You Yangs ranges. The existing sugar gum wind-rows are retained. Earth forms are shaped and moulded. Rock gabion sculptures and noise walls are constructed. Strong, bold plantings of colourful shrubs and avenue trees mark key arrival and departure points. The Corio Interchange is established as a gateway. Riparian environments along the creeks and rivers are reinstated. Existing viewsheds are enhanced by earthforms, retaining walls, structures and plantings that act to visually frame the open countryside and engage road users.

Geelong Road, Princes Freeway, Victoria

nature's garden

experience is vitiated
so many other lovers

the wilderness
by the presence of
of the wilderness

We often kill the things we love. This is the paradox of the wilderness experience: even mild tourist pressure on places of natural beauty erodes the possibility of direct personal engagement with their unspoilt qualities. The wilderness experience is vitiated by the presence of so many other lovers of the wilderness.

It is mediated by air-conditioned vehicles, interpretation centres, signs, walking tracks, viewing platforms. It is commodified by tourist promotional campaigns, sight-seeing tours, and the proliferation of off-road vehicles. By these means the natural landscape is tamed and co-opted. It remains beautiful but is neutralised and rendered safe by regulated, negotiated access. In our collective eagerness to experience the awe of nature, we literally trample it to death.

Pressure on places of natural beauty can only increase, and management by government agencies is essential. Even preserving places assimilates them into an invidious system of protection and conservation management that yearly becomes less able to withstand pressures of development, pollution and commercial exploitation. Yet the natural environment, and the wilderness particularly, are vital to the national heritage and ecology. In managing sites of natural beauty, inevitably there must be compromises between competing value systems: social, economic, political, environmental, aesthetic. Priorities are identified and ranked. Even the best outcomes will generate some dissatisfaction.

In the face of these contradictions, the landscape architect can hope to lead the experiential agenda. Paradoxically, this is best done by artificial means, by constructing visitors' preliminary experiences, preparing them, protecting them, propelling them along defined tracks and walkways, regulating their exposure. This is the best we can do to keep places of natural beauty at arm's length and preserve them by drawing a line around their wildness.

The Wilderness Experience

9.0

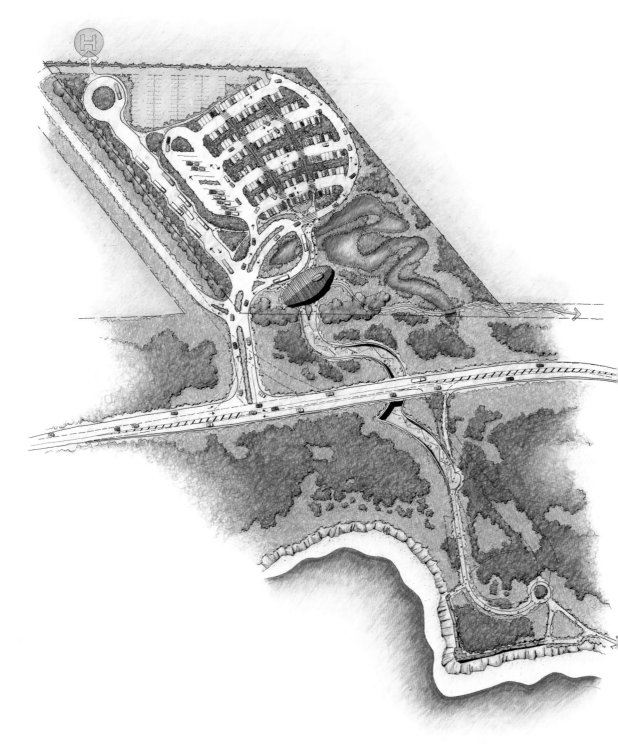

216_   Masterplanning, interpretation centre and car park, Twelve Apostles, Port Campbell, Victoria

9.1

The towering stone figures of the Twelve Apostles form one of the major tourist attractions along Victoria's dramatic south-western coastline. Lashed by surf, these rugged weathered monoliths jut straight out of the beach. The only visual interruption to the uninhabited stretch of coast is the snaking black road. But the amount of traffic drawing up along the rim of the cliff so people could admire the Twelve Apostles was destroying any sense of encountering nature, and turning the majestic bluff overlooking the sea into a ragged car park.

The decision to prevent vehicular access to the edge of the cliff and instead to locate a new car park well back from the road met with some local dismay: any built intervention in this powerful landscape was considered a violation of the wilderness. However, the laissez-faire parking policy could no longer be tolerated.

Tract's concept was for an interpretation centre – the building designed by Greg Burgess suggests an upturned boat – to be visible from the road, indicating to drivers approaching the Twelve Apostles where to turn off to park. The parking area – designed to accommodate tour buses as well as cars – is set in the open landscape. South-westerlies blow hard in winter, and trees have difficulty growing. Accordingly the landscape aesthetic is tough, reflecting the wide scale and raw terrain.

An old road and car park were torn up and replanted with native groundcover and shrubs, and a pedestrian pathway was defined that conducts visitors from the car park to the viewing platform at the edge of the cliff.

Materials were selected for their experiential qualities and to indicate that this is a special place: local limestone walls, timber planking, timber light pillars.

Rainwater run-off from the bitumen areas is treated before being discharged onto the land and ultimately into the sea. The run-off drains into polishing ponds that both purify the water and provide ornamentation. After the centre was constructed, run-off was found to be cleaner than when the site had been occupied by cattle.

The main principles were to remove the physically and visually damaging interventions from a breathtaking natural site, to provide legibility and safety for visitors, and to ensure environmentally sound management of the land.

Echo Point, Blue Mountains, New South Wales

9.2

Blue Mountains National Park, just a couple of hours' drive west of Sydney, has World Heritage listing. The Three Sisters formation has been a popular tourist destination since the days of the horse and buggy. Even today a drive through the rugged bush-clad Blue Mountains inspires wonder at the extent of the ranges and their comparative preservation from development. The Three Sisters is an impressive golden-orange sandstone outcrop that rises up from an escarpment, standing out against a backdrop of blue-green crags and valleys that extends to the far horizon. Despite proximity of a town and numerous immediate reminders of human presence, the majesty of the stone figures and their vertiginous setting still exert a powerful effect on modern imaginations, attracting scores of visitors daily.

Tract was principal consultant for the redevelopment of the public domain and visitor facilities for this national scenic attraction. The site has three areas: Echo Point, including the vehicular turnaround, parking, terraces, lookouts and the visitors' information centre; Darley Park; and Lilianfels Park.

Tract's design was developed within the framework of the Draft Plan of Management prepared by the Blue Mountains Council. This highlighted the importance of safe and rational access for visitors, the dramatic views, the need for infrastructure and facilities to complement the natural qualities, and minimising the impacts of visitors and urban development.

The paradox of the wilderness experience remains: the irresistible fascination of viewing/experiencing nature from the safety and comfort of a well-serviced tourist stop.

Healesville Sanctuary, Healesville, Victoria

9.3

Finding one's way around Healesville Sanctuary, a large rambling estate that incorporates wildlife exhibits, used to be a difficult challenge. To overcome the frustrations of getting lost and disoriented, and to cater for the variety of users – those visiting for just an hour or for a whole day – Tract devised a logical strategy for a 'yellow brick road' pathway system that allows all users to access the main exhibits in a one- to two-hour journey.

To create this logical path, Tract analysed the exhibits, infrastructure and visitor requirements, and prepared the detailed design and documentation of the primary path system, as well as modifications to the koala exhibit and the wombat enclosure, the design of picnic areas, furniture and signage, and perimeter planning, and the overall planting policy for the grounds.

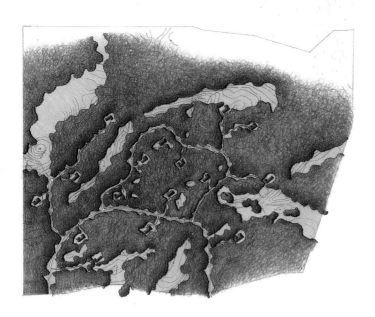

Otway Park, Cape Otway, Victoria

9.4

The site is a stunning one with an extensive native tree cover in a highly dissected stabilised dune environment. This dynamic and natural site influenced the design to merge into its setting. This design outcome was achieved as a result of comprehensive site analysis and site planning proposals that were prepared by Tract for a low-density rural cluster development for a bushland site of 70 hectares near Cape Otway (16 lots). Development plans for this land called for sensitive analysis and negotiations with a number of government agencies prior to receiving planning permission. Underlying the design outcome was the siting of each home to ensure privacy for all residents.

the garden

No matter a garden is not simply a universe in microcosm; to become immersed

how small or secret,
a fragment _____ but
_____ and implicitly
it invites the visitor
in this world

When we think of gardens, it is with an innate understanding that a garden exists as an encompassing, |contained, world-within-the-world. No matter how small or secret, a garden is not simply a fragment but a universe in microcosm; and implicitly it invites the visitor to become immersed in this world.

People are at the centre of a garden. It is created for human pleasure and appeals to nearly all the human senses, through shape and colour, perfume, texture, sound, temperature, and space. The garden does not extend or replicate raw nature but establishes a (literally) cultured realm concerned essentially with the human condition. The sights and spaces it creates afford refreshment, refuge, prospect delight.

Gardens are also designed as backdrops against which buildings are set off and events are staged. The country mansion set in manicured grounds, and the wedding party artfully posed in front of blossom trees, both rely equally on the powerful scenography of the garden, drawing on its magic to enhance their status. All parks and gardens, in a sense, descend from that original Eden of before the Fall, representing an unattainable ideal of carefree innocence. They are places to escape to, momentarily, and put aside mundane cares and responsibilities in order to be refreshed by a simpler, purer reality. A garden is time out.

10.0

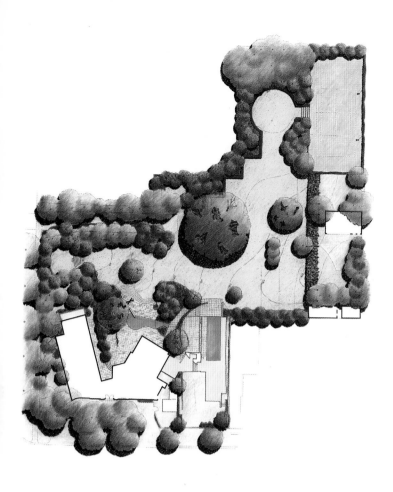

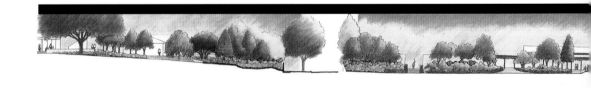

Private residence, Toorak, Victoria

This is a grand garden in an old suburb of Melbourne. The original garden established in the 1940s followed a modernist design theme. The new owners subsequently purchased an adjoining lot, expanding the area of the garden to 3 acres. Tract was commissioned first in 1978 to extend the terrace to the north on the adjoining land, and since then has been continuously engaged in the garden's development.

The idea of this garden is to make a private park, or to engender the feeling of wandering into a piece of park. The design defines spaces of various scales and proportions that offer contrasting sensations and experiences. The large open central spaces of clipped lawn have smaller hidden secret spaces located off them. Throughout the garden, juxtaposed contrasts heighten perceptions: high and low elements, open and sheltered spaces, sunny and shaded aspects, hard and soft landscape, native eucalypts and exotic trees, ordered and natural planting regimes.

The edges of spaces are important, holding the composition together. The precision of the low zigzagging hedges offsets the natural tree planting rising up behind. These tall trees give the impression that the forest extends forever.

The garden draws you in. It unfolds as you move through and encounter spaces, sculptures, views, places to linger. There are contained vistas as well as vistas that extend beyond the boundaries, amplifying the garden's perceived dimensions.

A rustic pergola was added in 1991, its scale sufficiently rugged to form a containing edge. The pergola supports a wisteria-draped arbour, a shaded, contemplative place to withdraw from the bright sunshine and stroll or sit in the cool.

The garden is for private enjoyment, and much of the owners' personalities is invested in its colours and references.

10.1

Private residence, Toorak, Victoria

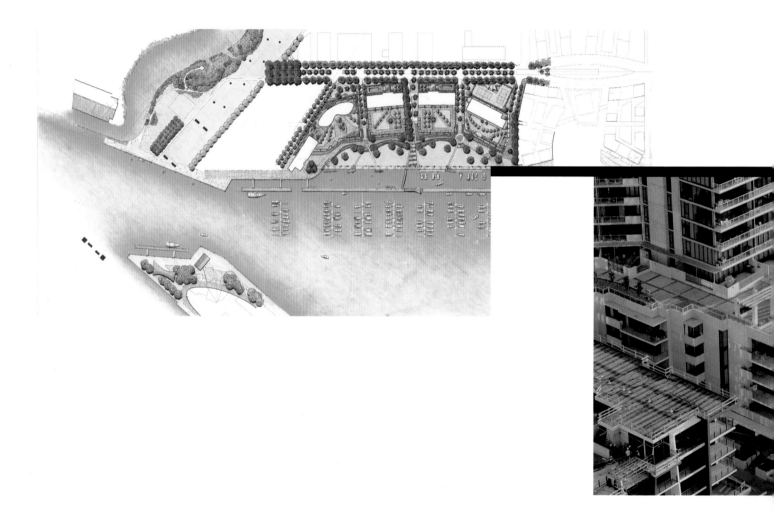

238_ Newquay (garden podiums), Docklands, Melbourne, Victoria

10.2

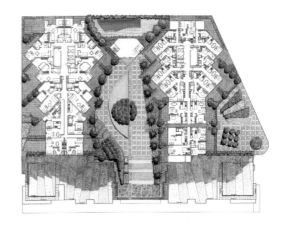

The garden podium levels of a new waterfront development in Docklands are vital in creating human-scaled places in an area characterised by its former huge industrial scale and which is still quite raw. The surrounding precincts of Docklands will take decades to complete, and opportunity for residents to interact and relax in a greener parks/garden environment could remain limited for some time.

The first level of design is shaping experiences, and here it is important that people feel comfortable rather than overwhelmed. The podium gardens soften the impact of the constructed environment and provide a refuge and connection with nature.

The gardens are viewed mainly from above from the surrounding tall buildings. Each podium becomes a pictorial plane onto which the garden projects an identity. The podium garden for the Nolan building, named after Australian painter Sir Sidney Nolan, suggests an abstract representation of the artist's best-known subject.

The Anchorage, Port Melbourne, Victoria

10.3

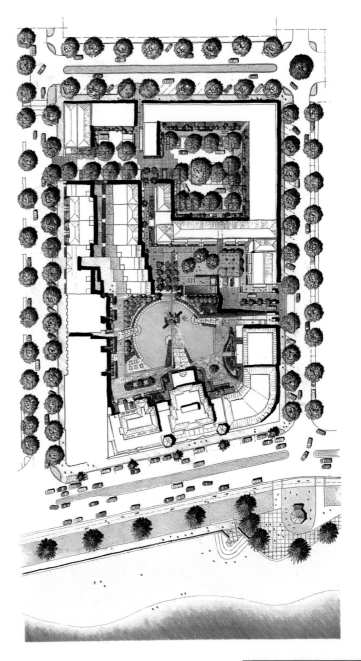

A former biscuit factory site occupying an entire block in Port Melbourne was developed as a medium- to high-density residential precinct. The desirable location by the bay is also close to the city. Existing heritage buildings were retained and new buildings incorporated to complete the block and establish inner lanes and streets. The exterior apartments are hard on the street, with no front gardens. Inner streets provide an address for apartments without street frontages. Cars are brought into the block yet it still feels like pedestrianised territory. The landscape treatment mostly serves as a visual amenity for apartments overlooking the open spaces and intimate garden courtyards.

Joondalup Park, Perth, Western Australia

10.4

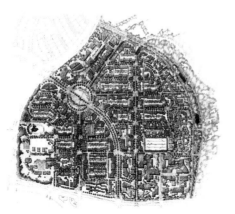

This is a bush park. An open space was allocated for the new town and a 5-hectare park excised from the existing bush. A system of low walls and paths defines circulation in the park and protects the defined areas of natural bushland where traffic is discouraged. People generally imagine that bushland does not need maintenance. However, irrigation is required for most of the year, and a lake provides water for sprinklers. In common with many public spaces built by developers, the park had a minimal budget. Its ultimate success depends on the developer's commitment to continuing maintenance and preserving the original design intention. The great value the park offers a new town not yet established is public amenity and identity.

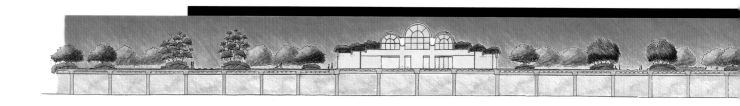

244_ **Perth bus terminal, Perth, Western Australia**

10.5

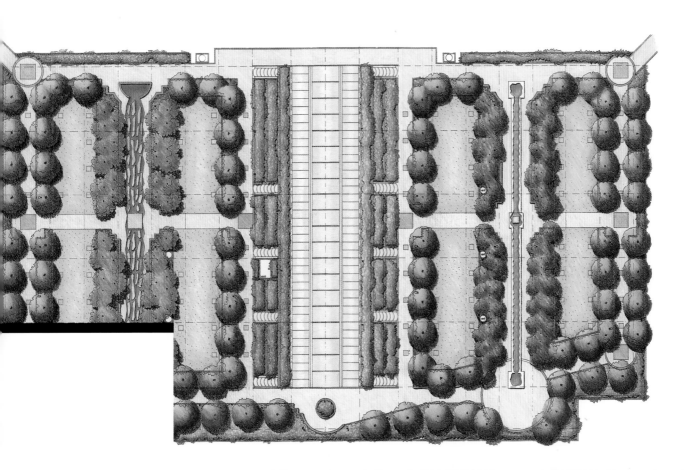

Tract was commissioned to design a roof garden on top of a 7-storey building in the city. Weight was a concern: it was important not to place too much soil on the roof. The climate oscillates between arid and wet. A structured grid was set up, and lawns and terraces defined. The purpose of the garden is ornamental, and it provides a pleasant setting for lunchtime visitors, and views from the nearby high-rise office buildings. A watercourse – suggesting the Fitzroy River – and fountain are refreshing features in the dry, hot conditions.

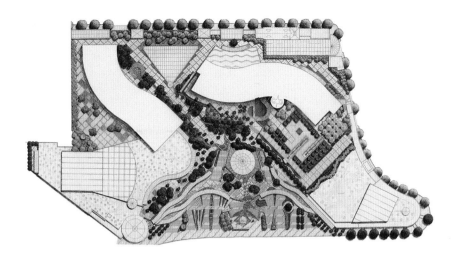

Star Casino, Sydney, New South Wales

The casino is located at Pyrmont on the
harbour. The architectural representation
of the sprawling artificial playground
complex emphasises fun and fantasy.
The intention behind the landscape
design is to present an array of Australian
landscapes: seaside, desert, tropical.
Most of the planting is located on top of
built structures, requiring major technical
interventions to allow the roof gardens
and podium landscapes to flourish.
Viewed from above, the gardens act as
pictorial carpets. Casino patrons can take
time out in them and enjoy the water
views across the harbour.

248_   TarraWarra Estate, Yarra Valley, Victoria

10.7

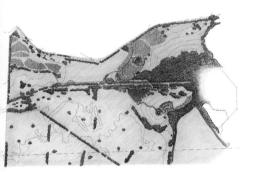

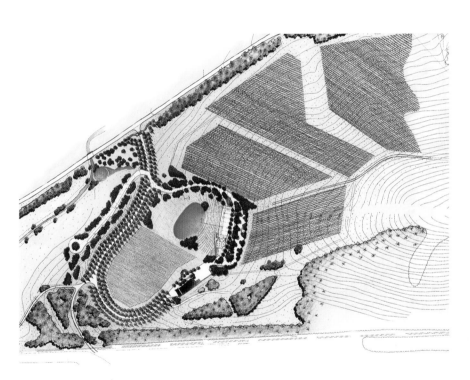

TarraWarra is a 365-hectare former dairy farm in the Yarra Valley, near Melbourne. The terrain includes rolling hills and 5 kilometres of river frontage. The estate has three functions: a private family retreat, a winery and art gallery open to the public, and a working farm.

The climate and landscape are tough. The family retreat on Home Hill has 360-degree views. A ha-ha wall prevents cattle from straying in. The family has located the house in a European setting and created a micro-climate amid the dry landscape, a landscape tactic that follows the classic pattern of immigrants establishing themselves in Australia. Native trees surrounding the exotic garden buffer the winds and offer protection against scorching summer conditions.

The entire property is designed, including the farm and the vineyard; it is landscape design on the scale of Capability Brown. The masterplan has been progressively implemented and constantly fine-tuned. Now maturing, it reflects a bucolic vision with a strong sense of the native bush. Initially there were few trees; however since the early 1980s more than 40,000 indigenous trees have been planted from seed collected on the property in order to maintain the pure regime of the area, rather than introduce eucalypts from elsewhere. The vast scale of the planting demanded persistence. Many seedlings died, and those that survived took time to take and mature. The benefits the

trees provide are varied: improved water run-off, stabilised creek banks, arrested erosion and silt loss, wind breaks, wildlife habitats, and increased ecological, economic viability for the farming and vineyard operations, as well as their aesthetic value.

Stone from an old quarry on the site is used for low walls and gateways. The main entry drive is lined with double rows of poplars, giving formal contrast and autumnal colour. The drive inscribes the land with a processional route to the winery and house. TarraWarra is experienced primarily from a moving car as a serial experience with a multitude of views. Sculptures are situated in the topography in outdoor 'rooms' accessed from the road. The property can be considered as a 'house', with

the road a corridor giving onto various rooms, each containing furniture/ sculpture. On approaching the house, a meadmore is encountered, reflected in the lake, and views of the house on the hill.

Duration is implicit in landscape design: it takes decades and sometimes generations to mature, and success depends on maintenance and fine-tuning. TarraWarra represents a rare opportunity to create, maintain and refine the landscape.

A new public gallery was opened in 2003 to house the owners' extensive collection of contemporary Australian art.

landscape architecture

gives the utilitarian
a scenic vision

Landscape Architecture

1 Frederick Law Olmsted
2 JB Jackson
3 Albert Fein
4 Ian McHarg
6 Kevin Lynch

5 Harvard University

Modernism

7 Kiley, Rose, Eckbo
8 Walter Gropius
9 Sasaki Walker

Education

10 Melbourne University Professional fellows
10 RMIT First professional landscape architecture course
11 Early practitioners

10 Rodney Wulff and Steve Calhoun

20 Tract Consultants

Early Australian landscape school

12 Edna Walling and Ellis Stones

13 David Yencken and Howard McCorkell

Planning

14 Programmes of the Department of Urban and Regional Development
15 Peter Hall
16 Sir Patrick Geddes
17 William H Whyte
18 Ebenezer Howard
19 Lewis Mumford

Tract influences

7 Dan Kiley, James Rose and Garrett Eckbo
As students at Harvard in 1934, they were taught in the Beaux Arts style. They wrote and published a manifesto urging that landscape architecture embrace modernism. Each became a well-known modernist landscape architect. Dan Kiley is still practising at the time of writing.

8 Walter Gropius
A leading force in the Bauhaus movement, fled to America from Nazi Germany in the 1930s, became the head of the architecture programme at Harvard from the late 1930s to late 1970s.

9 Sasaki Walker
Sasaki Walker was the first large corporate landscape architectural office in America, coming into prominence during the 1960s. Hideo Sasaki was chairman of the landscape architectural programme at Harvard during the 1950s and 1960s. He advocated collaboration with architects, planners, engineers and environmentalists. Peter Walker moved to San Francisco in the 1960s to run Sasaki Walker, renamed the SWA Group, on the West Coast. Peter returned to Harvard to Chair the Department in the mid-1970s and started a firm with Martha Schwartz that became known for its avant-garde work in the 1980s and 1990s. Peter now runs Peter Walker and Partners and started Space Maker Press, specialising in publishing the work of landscape architects. Hideo Sasaki and Peter Walker were co-recipients of the Harvard Landscape Architecture Department's Centenary Gold Medal.

10 Rodney Wulff and Steve Calhoun
Rodney Wulff, an Australian educated at Oregon, Harvard and Cornell, joined Tract in 1974. Steve Calhoun worked for Sasaki Walker for five years before joining

14 Programmes of the Department of Urban and Regional Development (DURD) 1972–1975
The Department of Urban and Regional Development was established by the Whitlam government in 1972 to promote regional development of Australia, relieving growth pressures on capital cities and encouraging regional employment.

15 Peter Hall
British planner Peter Hall was professor of planning at the Bartlett School of Architecture and Planning, University College, London. Hall, throughout his career as a planner, has written and edited nearly thirty books on urban and regional planning.

16 Patrick Geddes
It is argued by some that Geddes introduced regional planning to the Western world and was perhaps the first among contemporary planners to sense the need for planning larger areas, especially around urban centres. With a background in biology and geography, Geddes attempted to achieve a balance between natural and human environments.

1 Frederick Law Olmsted

Grandfather of modern landscape architecture. Created many park systems throughout America between the 1850s and 1900. Designed Central Park in New York City and wrote extensively on social and environmental issues. Son Frederick Law Olmsted Jr founded first course in landscape architecture at Harvard University in 1901.

2 JB Jackson

Lectured at Harvard and Berkeley on the cultural landscape, between the 1960s and 1980s. Wrote many books including *A Sense of Place, A Sense of Time*.

3 Albert Fein

Social historian who wrote a book and lectured at Harvard on Frederick Law Olmsted's social philosophy.

4 Ian McHarg

A graduate of Harvard who became famous for leading a crusade for environmental planning. Wrote *Design with Nature* during the 1960s. Chairman of Landscape Architecture and Planning Department at University of Pennsylvania.

5 Harvard University

Followed on from McHarg's work with the introduction of computer modelling of environmental data. Charles Harris was chairman of Landscape Architecture programme 1960s–1970s. Steinitz and Way introduced advanced land analysis techniques through aerial photographic interpretation.

6 Kevin Lynch

Professor of Urban Design at MIT 1960s–1970s. His books and lectures (taken by many Harvard landscape architectural students) were profoundly influential. Wrote *Site Planning* and *Image of the City*.

11 Early practitioners

Graham Bentley, Chris Dance, George Gallagher, Andrea McDonald, Barry Murphy and Stuart Pullyblank. Landscape practitioners who were in the first RMIT course taught by Wulff and Calhoun. They all currently run substantial offices throughout Australia.

12 Edna Walling and Ellis Stones

Edna Walling was one of the first professional landscape designers in Australia. Her work derived from the English garden tradition popularised by Gertrude Jekyll. Ellis Stones worked for Edna in the beginning of his career. Ellis extended Edna's work with the use of Australian plants and less formality to popularise the Australian Bush School.

13 David Yencken and Howard McCorkell

David Yencken founded Tract Consultants in the early 1970s as an extension of Merchant Builders, a building company he founded with John Ridge that was the first of its kind to offer high-quality architecturally designed homes with an Australian character. A renaissance figure of the 1960s, 1970s and 1980s, David was chairman of the Australian Heritage Commission, secretary of the Ministry of Planning and chairman of the Australian Conservation Foundation. He held the Dame Elisabeth Murdoch Chair of Landscape Architecture at Melbourne University during the 1990s. One of the three founding directors of Tract with Rodney Wulff and Steve Calhoun, Howard brought complementary strategic planning skills. With a lifelong interest in residential planning, Howard was a leading advocate for cluster housing. He retired from the practice in 1996.

17 William H Whyte

A graduate of Princeton, Whyte spent many years walking the streets of New York studying pedestrians and their interaction with urban spaces. For this he is considered a mentor of projects for public spaces.

18 Ebenezer Howard

Ebenezer Howard was a utopian planner during the mid-nineteenth century. In 1898 he introduced the Garden City idea to England in an attempt to plan healthy and attractive cities that were self-sustaining.

19 Lewis Mumford

A professor at Stanford University, Mumford is renowned for his writings on cities, architecture, technology, literature and modern life. His writing ranged freely and appealed to a wide variety of people including writers, artists, city planners, architects, philosophers, historians and archaeologists.

20 Tract Consultants

In addition to Rodney Wulff and Steve Calhoun, the current directors of Tract include:

Mike Stokes, who joined Tract in Melbourne, 1984; George Gallagher (1979) and Julie Lee established the Sydney office, 1988; Nevan Wadeson joined Tract, 1992, ultimately to replace Howard McCorkell as Tract's planning director in 1995; Stephen White joined Tract in Brisbane, 1994, and became a director in 2001.

Mark Doonar & Associates merged with Tract in 2001 to establish a planning presence in Queensland, and Mark became a director in 2003. Tract (WA) under Stuart Pullyblank's direction was established as an associate office to Tract in 1992 and continues to work in association.

Kevin Abbott
Glenys Adams
Coreen Addison
Nathan Alexander
Mike Allen
Jeffrey Allott
Drew Anderson
Tate Anderson
Nikolee Ansell
Sharon Apgar
Gilbert Arnold
Matthew Arthur
Lyn Bain
Ann Barber
Andrew Baronski
Peter Barrett
John Bedford
Helen Bell
Pali Bell
Don Bergman
Andrew Biacsi
Timothy Biles
Stephen Birrell
Joby Blackman
Joanne Blackmore
Laurence Blyton
Ana Borovic
Vaughn Bowden
Suzanne Boxall
Suzy Boyd
Mark Brandon
Scott Burrows
Joanna Bush
Paul Buxton
Chris Byrne
Sharon Cain
Joanne Calder
Steve Calhoun
Emma Carr
Cathy Chalmers
Juliet Chaston
Anna Chauvel
Linda Cheong
Robert Choucroun
Graeme Coggins
Peter Cole
Marc Collister
Damien Colombo
Andrew Comer
Rachel Condon
Travis Conway
Noel Corkery

Suzie Patrick
John Patrick
Kate Patterson
Michelle Pearson
Damien Pericles
Ross Perrott
Leesa Perta
Anna Peters
Robert Petrilli
Angela Pidgeon
Don Pollock
Mara Porcellato (Bridge)
Dominic Powell
Tad Powers
Ben Price
Clarissa Puertas
Carson Pullyblank
Hayley Pullyblank
Jenny Pullyblank
Stuart Pullyblank
Sean Quinn
Jenny Rayment
Chris Razzell
Kim Reddrop
Gloria Regalado
Mark Reilly
Grant Revell
Justine Roberts
Andrew Robertson
Jason Robinson
Matthew Rogers
Yvonne Rust
Chad Ryan
Bernd Sawatsky
Justin Schreuder
Vicki Sciberras
Paul Scroggie
Andrae Seredenko
Daniel Sharp
Jane Shepherd
Alicia Shum
Julian Simeoni
Katherine Simmons
Sidh Sintusingha
Michael Siu
Justin Slater

Marion Fredriksson
Hamish Freeman
George Gallagher
Richard Garnham
George Gentner
Michael Gerner
Miranda Gibson
Alison Glynn
Andrea Grace
Mal Graham
Stuart Green
Sarah Gregg
Peter Grose
Julie Hallyburton
Jacqueline Hanna
Frank Hanson
Pollyanna Harvey
Gerard Healy
Cathy Heggen
Tanya Henry
Greg Hocking
Fiona Hoffmann
Sarah Hopkins
Jamie Hopwood
Jane Horgan
Nick Hunt
Melinda Hunt
Jafri Hussain
Bettina Jacoby
Renee Jezard
Michael Juttner
Samantha Keeling
Elizabeth Kenny
Michael Kerr
Fiona Kidman
Andree King (White)
Sonia Kirby
Russell Kosko
Peter Krstic
Susie Kumar

top row:
Rodney Wulff
Steve Calhoun
George Gallagher
Michael Stokes
Julie Lee
Nevan Wadeson
Stephen White
Mark Doonar

middle row:
George Gentner
Deiter Lim
Andrew Robertson
Richard Garnham
Matthew Easton
Melissa Dunlop (Wain)
Alison Glynn
Sally McDonald
Sue Owens

bottom row:
Brett Davis
Justin Slater
Janice Foster
Ashley Sutch
Janis Fisher

Representative personnel_Current employees as well as those usually with a minimum of one year at Tract

258_

Michael Cowled
Doug Cromb
Kevin Cronin
Christopher Dance
Brett Davis
Paul Dawes
Natalie Demarte
Helen Dickson
Sarah Donnelley
Mark Doonar
Ben Doughty
Melissa Dunlop (Wain)
Karen Dunmall
Rachel Dwyer
Matthew Easton
Dennis Eiszele
Sarah Emons
Penny Faul
Emma Ferguson
Janis Fischer
Michael Ford
Janice Foster
Sue Franco (Ozanne)

Zinta Lazdins
Gini Lee
Julie Lee
Tom Lenigas
Christine Leonard
Lorne Leonard
Rebecca Leyshan
Andrew Lilleyman
Deiter Lim
Chris Lingard
Heidi Llewellyn
Joanne Lloyd
Xiao Liu Luo
Chris Mahoney
Michelle Maiolo
Sally Malone
David Martinus
Noel Matthews
Joanna Matthews (McMeekin)
Carol McConville
Howard McCorkell
Sally McDonald
Anthony McEwan
Chris Melsom
Tanya Metcher
Martin Mileham
John Minnikin
Ross Montgomery
Ben Morieson
Fiona Moss
Andrew Moyle
Barry Murphy
Tony Murphy
Michael Natoli
Jenny Neales
Christina Nicholson
Antony Nobbs
David O'Brien
Simon O'Callaghan
Julian O'Connell
Claire Ogston
Jane Osborn
Andrew Osborne
Lyndel Osborne
Michael Ostdick
Sue Owens
Rachel Palmer
Christine Pantazis

Elisabeth Smarrelli
Ali Smith
Pru Smith
Amy Sorger (Johnston)
Tina Souvlis
Justin Staggard
Jennifer Stanwix (Futcher)
Jennifer Stewart
Jermey Stewart
Michael Stokes
Michele Stynes
Andrew Suggitt
Louise Sureda
Ashley Sutch
Nick Taylor
Kevin Taylor
David Telfer
Jodie Tennyson
Adam Terrill
Richard Thomas
Sam Thompson
Andrew Tomlins
Annghi Tran
Yen Trinh
Ian Tucker
John Tuzee
Joel Twining
Teresa Vega
Frances Vernon
Nils Vesk
Khalid Vidot
Halima Vos
Julie Wade
Nevan Wadeson
Paul Wakelam
Lisa Walker
Melissa Warren
Helen Wellman (Balfe)
Alistair Wenn
Stephanie Wharton
Stephen White
Justine Williams
Christine Withers
Liam Wood
Jenny Wright
John Wright
Philip Wulff
Rodney Wulff
Steve York
Marlon Zeibell

Every effort has been made to include past employees with over one year's service. We apologise if anyone has been inadvertently omitted.

Competitions

Tract has achieved unequalled success in competitions, including:

1980 The Grange (a medium-density residential community in Sydney)
1981 Newcastle foreshore competition
1983 Sandridge City (Station Pier, Port Melbourne)
1985 Palm Plaza (pedestrian mall, Dandenong)
1990 Jupiters Casino (redevelopment of Queens Park, Brisbane)
1992 Convention Centre, Brisbane
1994 Convention Centre, Cairns
1995 Cathedral Place Park Hyatt, Parliamentary Precinct, Melbourne
1995 Circular Quay urban design competition
1996 Deakin University Central Courtyard, Burwood
1997 Manly Wharf and transport interchange, Sydney
1997 Rockhampton CBD revitalisation project, Queensland
1998 QUT Environment Courtyard, Brisbane
1998 Cairns Esplanade, Queensland
1999 University of Adelaide, 125th Anniversary

AILA Awards

Tract has won an award in every National AILA award ceremony it has entered since the awards' inception in 1986. Awards include:

1986 Vermont Park, Melbourne – AILA Award and the RAIA Robin Boyd Environmental Medal (Merchant Builders)
1986 Summer School
1988 Healesville Sanctuary, Victoria
1988 Government Precinct, Brisbane
1988 Australian Chancery complex
1988 Scroggie residence, Melbourne
1990 Ballarat Mall, Victoria
1990 ICI House, Melbourne
1990 National Tennis Centre, Melbourne
1992 Palm Plaza, Melbourne
1994 Laguna Quays, Queensland
1996 TarraWarra Vineyard, Victoria
1997 Queensland University of Technology, Main Drive
1997 Portland foreshore and CBD masterplans
1998 Eastern Freeway extension
1998 Private residence, Toorak, Victoria
1998 Deakin University Central Courtyard, Burwood – Award of Excellence
2002 Queensland University of Technology, Gardens Point Campus, Brisbane
2002 Manly Wharf interchange, Sydney
2003 Cairns Esplanade – Queensland Excellence Award in Design
2003 Twelve Apostles Visitor Centre, Port Campbell, Victoria
2003 The Mansion at Werribee Park, Victoria
2003 Bunurong Memorial Park, Victoria
2003 Commonwealth Games Village, Royal Park, Victoria

Awards and winning competitions

Other professional awards

Tract has been a key member of RAIA and other professional groups' award-winning teams. Awards include:

1986   Prahran Market, Gunn Hayball – RAIA

1988   Waverley Municipal offices, Harry Seidler & Associates – RAIA

1989   Newcastle Harbour foreshore redevelopment – RAIA Lloyd Rees Urban Design Award

1990   Southbank promenade, Denton Corker Marshall – RAIA

1990   Medium-density housing in association with Swinburne University

1991   Trinity Grammar Watson Bld stage one, Crone Ross Architects – RAIA National Award

1992   Trinity Grammar Watson Bld stage two, Crone Ross Architects – RAIA

1992   QV1 Perth, Harry Seidler & Associates – RAIA

1992   MCG Great Southern Stand, Daryl Jackson/Tompkins, Shaw & Evans Architects – RAIA National Award

1993   Trinity Grammar Chapel, Crone Ross Architects – RAIA

1995   Residential Zone Review – RAPI

2002   The Mansion at Werribee Park, Wood Marsh Architects

2002   Asia Centre University of Melbourne, Nation Fender Katsalidis Architects

2003   Trinity Grammar Science Building, Crone Ross Architects – RAIA

2003   NewQuay restaurant precinct, MGS Architects

2003   NewQuay residential/commercial, Fender Katsalidis

Tract has played a significant part in the following projects, which have won awards in the Royal Australian Planning Institute (RAPI) and Planning Institute of Australia (PIA) annual Awards for Excellence, including:

2002   Queensland University of Technology, Gardens Point Campus masterplan – Urban Design Award, Queensland

2002   Capalaba bus station – Urban Design Certificate of Merit, Queensland

2003   Cairns Esplanade – Urban Design Award, Queensland

2003   Lake masterplan, Wuxi China – International Projects Certificate of Merit, Queensland

Tract has played a significant part in the following projects, which have won awards in the Urban Development Institute of Australia annual Awards for Excellence, including:

1998   Deakin University Central Courtyard, Burwood – Award of Excellence, Best Project in Australia AILA Award and Building Design Professions (RAIA, ACAA, AILA, RAPI, ACEA, AIQS, IEA and RAIA) National Urban Design Award

2000   Lynbrook Estate – Victoria, Carrington Estate, Victoria

2001   The Cascades, Victoria

2002   Twin Water resort, Sunshine Coast, Queensland

2003   Ellington apartments, Brisbane, Queensland

2003   Cairns Esplanade, Queensland – The Australian Award for Urban Design Excellence (RAIA, PIA and AILA – Best Project in Australia) National Urban Design Awards

Acknowledgements and references

(at the time of carrying out the project)

262_

Acknowledgements and references

Chapter 8: The Road

Project	Page	Client / Architect / Contractor	Photographer
Eastern Freeway extension, Melbourne, Victoria	194	VicRoads / Wood Marsh Architects	John Gollings Photographer
	196		
South East Transit Busway, Brisbane, Queensland	198	Queensland Transport / Cottee Parker Architects	Scott Burrows, Aperture Photography
	200		Scott Burrows, Aperture Photography
	202		Scott Burrows, Aperture Photography
Urban freeways, Melbourne, Sydney, Brisbane	204	Leighton Contractors / Maunsell / GHD	Interlink
South-Eastern Freeway (Monash Freeway) Melbourne		VicRoads	
M5, Sydney motorway		Leighton	
Gateway motorway extension, Queensland		Thiess Contractors	
Sydney International Airport, Sydney, New South Wales	206	Sydney Airports Corporation / Cocks Carmichael Architects	
Geelong Road, Princes Freeway, Victoria	208	Leighton Contractors for VicRoads	

Chapter 9: Nature's Garden

Project	Page	Client / Architect / Contractor	Photographer
Twelve Apostles, Port Campbell, Victoria	216		John Gollings Photographer
	218		John Gollings Photographer
Echo Point, Blue Mountains, New South Wales	220	Blue Mountains City Council / Ancher Mortlock Woolley Architects	Brett Cornish Photography
	222		Brett Cornish Photography
Healesville Sanctuary, Healesville, Victoria	224	Zoological Board of Victoria / John Herner	John Gollings Photographer
	226		John Gollings Photographer
Otway Park, Cape Otway, Victoria	228		

Chapter 10: The Garden

Project	Page	Client / Architect / Contractor	Photographer
Private residence, Toorak, Victoria	234		John Gollings Photographer
	236		John Gollings Photographer
NewQuay (garden podiums), Docklands, Melbourne, Victoria	238	MAB Docklands Pty Ltd / Nation Fender Katsalidis	
The Anchorage, Port Melbourne, Victoria	240	MAB Pty Ltd / Plus Architecture Pty Ltd / SJB Architects	
Joondalup Park, Perth, Western Australia	242	Joondalup Authority	Peter Bennetts courtesy of Catherin Bull*
Perth bus terminal, Perth, Western Australia	244	Western Australian Department of Transport	
Star Casino, Sydney, New South Wales	246	Star Casino / Cox Architects / BJ O'Neil Engineers	John Gollings Photographer
TarraWarra Estate, Yarra Valley, Victoria	248	Private client / Gunn Williams Fender Architects / BJ O'Neil Engineers	
	250	Allan Powell Architects and Irwin Alsop Group	John Gollings Photographer
	252		John Gollings Photographer

* Courtesy of Professor Catherin Bull, Elisabeth Murdoch Chair of Landscape Architecture, University of Melbourne. From her recent book 'New Conversations with an Old Landscape', 2002. Photography by Peter Bennetts